Attitudes and Language

Multilingual Matters

About Translation
    PETER NEWMARK
The Acquisition of Irish
    MAIRE OWENS
Breaking the Boundaries
    EUAN REID and HANS H. REICH (eds)
Continuing to Think
    BARRIE WADE and PAMELA SOUTER
Critical Theory and Classroom Talk
    ROBERT YOUNG
Cultural Studies and Language Learning
    M. BYRAM, V. ESARTE-SARRIES and S. TAYLOR
English in Wales: Diversity, Conflict and Change
    N. COUPLAND in association with A. THOMAS (eds)
Foreign/Second Language Pedagogy Research
    R.PHILLIPSON, E. KELLERMAN, L. SELINKER,
    M. SHARWOOD SMITH and M. SWAIN (eds)
Investigating Cultural Studies in Foreign Language Teaching
    M. BYRAM and V. ESARTE-SARRIES
Key Issues in Bilingualism and Bilingual Education
    COLIN BAKER
Language, Culture and Cognition
    LILLIAM MALAVÉ and GEORGES DUQUETTE (eds)
Language in Education in Africa
    CASMIR M. RUBAGUMYA (ed.)
Language Policy Across the Curriculum
    DAVID CORSON
Mediating Languages and Cultures
    D. BUTTJES and N. BYRAM (eds)
Multilingualism in India
    D. P. PATTANAYAK (ed)
New Zealand Ways of Speaking English
    A. BELL and J. HOLMES (eds)
Our Own Language
    GABRIELLE MAGUIRE
Reversing Language Shift
    JOSHUA A. FISHMAN
Second Language Acquisition and Language Pedagogy
    ROD ELLIS
System in Black Language
    DAVID SUTCLIFFE with JOHN FIGUEROA
The Use of Welsh: A Contribution to Sociolinguistics
    MARTIN J. BALL (ed.)

Please contact us for the latest book information:
Multilingual Matters Ltd,
Frankfurt Lodge, Clevedon Hall,
Victoria Road, Clevedon,
Avon BS21 7SJ, England

Lynne Díaz-Rico

MULTILINGUAL MATTERS 83
Series Editor: Derrick Sharp

Attitudes and Language

Colin Baker

MULTILINGUAL MATTERS LTD
Clevedon • Philiadelphia • Adelaide

Library of Congress Cataloging in Publication Data

Baker, Colin, 1949-
Attitudes and Language/Colin Baker
p. cm. (Multilingual Matters: 83)
Includes bibliographical references and index
1. Language awareness. 2. Attitude (Psychology). 3. Bilingualism.
I. Title. II. Series: Multilingual Matters (Series): 83.
P120.L34B35   1992
404'.2   dc 20

British Library Cataloguing in Publication Data

A CIP catalogue record for this book is available from the British Library.

ISBN 1-85359-143-2 (hbk)
ISBN 1-85359-142-4 (pbk)

Multilingual Matters Ltd

UK: Frankfurt Lodge, Clevedon Hall, Victoria Road, Clevedon, Avon BS21 7SJ.
USA: 1900 Frost Road, Suite 101, Bristol, PA 19007, USA.
Australia: P.O. Box 6025, 83 Gilles Street, Adelaide, SA 5000, Australia.

Printed and bound in Great Britain by WBC Print Ltd, Bridgend.

For Derrick Sharp

Derrick Sharp co-founded the Multilingual Matters Book Series. Academics tend to believe it is they who push forward the frontiers of bilingualism. This belief may hide the contribution of those who risked a publishing venture around multilingualism. The effect of Derrick and others who have promoted the MLM Series is not to be underestimated. Through his own books and through cultivating the topic of bilingualism through the Multilingual Matters Series, Derrick has given great service to the study and practice of bilingualism and bilingual education.

Colin Baker

Colin has very kindly given us the opportunity of adding our thanks to Derrick at this point. We take particular pleasure in doing so, as a book of this nature typifies the strength of the teamwork that Derrick brought to Multilingual Matters Ltd.

When we started the company and were looking for people to work with, nearly all roads led to Derrick. His contribution, directly in the *Journal of Multilingual and Multicultural Development* and in the Multilingual Matters Book Series, and indirectly in our other journals and books, should be seen as the single most important factor in placing the company where it is today.

Now Derrick is retiring (again!) it is a comfort to know that he will still be advising us on company policy and will be editing the Multilingual Matters Series for some time to come.

To put it simply — Thanks, Derrick, from

Berni, Kathryn, Ken, Marjukka, Mike and Sheila
(the Multilingual Matters office team)

Contents

Acknowledgements   ix
Prologue
    Introduction   1
    Plan of the Book   4

1 Attitudes and Language: Foundational Issues
    Introduction   8
    The Importance of Attitudes   9
    The Nature of an Attitude   10
    Attitude as Input and Output   12
    The Three Components of Attitude   12
    Attitude and Related Terms   13
    Attitudes and Behaviour   15
    The Measurement of Attitudes   17
    Conclusions   20

2 The Origin of Language Attitudes
    Introduction   22
    Evolving a Systems Model of Language Attitudes   23
    Problems and Issues   27
    The Nature of Language Attitudes   29
    Instrumental and Integrative Attitudes   31
    Research into Integrative and Instrumental Attitudes   33
    Further Directions in Research   35
    Gardner's Socio-Educational Model   38
    Research into the Determinants of Language Attitudes   41
    Summary   46

3 Attitudes and Language : A Research Perspective
    Introduction   48
    Choice of Variables   49
    The Measurement of the Variables   51
    The Passage of the Research   55
    Scaling   55
    Reliabilities   59

Initial Explorations   59
The Model   68
Summary   74

4 Attitudes to Bilingualism
Introduction   76
The Characterisation of Attitude to Bilingualism   79
The Development of an Attitude to Bilingualism Scale   81
The Uniqueness of Attitude to Bilingualism   84
The Utility of Attitude to Bilingualism   88
A Model of Attitude to Bilingualism   92
Conclusions   96

5 Language and Attitude Change
Introduction   97
Historical Perspective   97
Theories of Attitude Change   99
Age Changes   106
Dramatic Experiences   106
Community Effects   107
Parental Effects   109
Peer Group Effects   109
Institutional Effects   110
Mass Media Effects   110
Rituals   111
Situational Effects   111
Summary and Conclusion   112

6 Language and Attitude Change: A Research Perspective
Introduction and Aims   114
Background   115
Issue One   117
Issue Two   120
Issue Three   124
Issue Four   126
Summary   131

Postscript: Perspectives and Prospects   133
Appendix 1: The Research Instruments   138
Appendix 2: Technical Details of the Research   152
References   164
Index   171

Acknowledgements

Surrounded by friends and colleagues whose co-operation and help have been exemplary, the passage of this book has been a pleasure. While writing and re-drafting were often conducted in monastic silence, the assistance of the people listed below ensured a sociable back-up.

At the start of the venture, permission to conduct the research was given by two Directors of Education and three Headteachers. The three busy Headteachers not only gave me access to their classrooms, but were generous in assistance. The hospitality received and friendliness shown made the research a pleasure. The research would not have been possible without 800 pupils taking time and effort to complete the attitude questionnaires. Gratitude is expressed to these teenagers who provided the raw data.

When the research instruments were constructed, a gentle, gracious and generous mentor stepped in to translate the tests into Welsh. Dr. Bryn Davies taught me Comparative Education as an undergraduate. The meticulous support shown then has been reproduced a hundred times since. Diolch yn fawr iawn, B.L.. Then, when the data analysis was proceeding, Dr. Nick Ellis of the Psychology Department, UCNW, offered crucial advice on the intricacies of LISREL. When the first drafts were completed, a popular social psychologist gave me advice, gentle criticism and plenty of reinforcement. As an enthusiastic and inspiring lecturer, Alun Waddon opened the door of social psychology to me as an undergraduate. He revealed a room full of surprises and splendour. A *tour de force*, still being provided to generations of undergraduates, initiated my interest in attitude theory and research. Without Alun igniting that first spark, this book may never have been written. The book would never have been completed without the kindness and encouragement of my Head of Department, Professor Iolo Wyn Williams. He provided the facilitative backing that enabled the creation of this text.

The financial support of the Economic and Social Research Council (ESRC) is gratefully acknowledged. The research reported in parts of this book was funded by ESRC award number R000221045. Certain paragraphs from my *Key Issues in Bilingualism and Bilingual Education* have been re-utilised in this book where theory is featured.

The typing of the handwritten drafts was skilfully undertaken by my favourite word processor. The applause does not go to the mighty micro-computers, nor to the splendid software. It goes to Dilys Parry. She is the one who turns ugly script into handsome print outs. She makes us all feel we are doing her a favour by giving her mountains of illegible script. Never ruffled, always cheerful, gentle and humorous, she convinces me of angels on earth.

Thanks go to all the members of my academic, extended and nuclear family whose generous attitude to me is undeserved. The first draft of this book was written during a time of family loss; she whose attitude to the end of the illness and the day of promotion taught something that can never be learnt from a book.

The draft was also read in entirety by Derrick Sharp, the most important father of language attitude research in Wales. There can be no other editor so helpful, encouraging, thoughtful, sensitive and diplomatic. The production of the book was made a pleasure by such a positive, open and skilful approach. Diolch, yet again, Derrick; to you this book is dedicated.

Prologue

Introduction

This book brings together two major concepts that are both interdisciplinary and international. The notion of attitudes has a place in psychology, sociology, anthropology, education, history, human geography and creative arts. Similarly bilingualism and minority languages are not topics confined to linguistics or language studies, but enter debates in education, psychology, geography, politics, sociology, law and anthropology. The bringing together of attitudes and bilingualism was previously considered when writing *Key Issues in Bilingualism and Bilingual Education* (1988). It became clear that there was a strong research tradition connecting bilingualism with intelligence and cognitive functioning. Research on bilingual education was similarly not scarce. These areas still demand further research, especially with regard to contemporary research interests in information processing and school effectiveness. In contrast, the tradition connecting attitudes and motivation with bilingualism and minority languages seemed less strong. The importance of attitudes in bilingualism as an individual or societal phenomenon seems latently assumed in many psychological, sociological, geolinguistic and educational writings. The amount of explicit theory and research on the topic appears surprisingly small.

Five particular deficiencies may be identified in writings on attitudes and language. The first deficiency is the relationship between general attitude theory and attitude research on the one hand, and research specifically on language attitudes on the other hand. The latter seems rarely to have been informed by the former. When reviewing attitude and language research in *Key Issues in Bilingualism and Bilingual Education*, it became apparent that only a small number of researchers or authors demonstrated awareness of attitude theory. As will be shown in Chapter 1, attitude theory has developed significantly in the last 60 years, and evolved through at least three pivotal changes (McQuire, 1985). The literature on language attitudes seems not to draw upon nor reflect this evolution of theory. Much language attitude literature is atheoretical. Therefore the many insights to be gained from attitude theory are missing. This book aims partly to rectify

1

the situation, by explicitly grounding attitudes to language and bilingualism in attitude theory and general attitude research.

The second deficiency noticed when reviewing language attitude research was the almost total absence of references to attitude change. Since attitude change has been a dominant and well researched issue in social psychology, and since much writing on minority languages is tacitly or overtly about language decay or restoration, connecting attitude change theory and language attitudes seems very desirable. Perhaps due to the lack of social psychologists interested in language and bilingualism (especially relative to the interest of sociologists and linguists), the relevance and power of attitude change theory and research to language change is noticeably absent. One chapter of this book attempts to rectify this situation. A further chapter illustrates attitude change research in terms of languages and bilingualism.

The third deficiency noticed when reviewing language attitude research was the technical deficiencies in the measurement of attitudes and subsequent statistical analysis. Attitude measures have too frequently been constructed without concern for reliability and multidimensionality. Relating attitude measures to other variables has then tended to be bivariate rather than multivariate. The availability of multivariate statistical tools (e.g. cluster analysis, structural equation modelling, discriminant function analysis) allows not only for increased sophistication over simple bivariate significance testing, but for more refined and informed conclusions. Model building and model testing by log-linear analysis and structural equation modelling, while possessing inherent dangers and limitations, is a development that moves us from the over-simplicity of early language attitudes research. While no universal panacea and not to be used solely and indiscriminately, the positing and testing of models allows the building of complex relationships defining the relative size of indirect and direct effects. This book, through a piece of research in Wales, illustrates the process of multidimensional attitude measurement plus the building and testing models of attitudes and attitude change.

The fourth deficiency revealed in the attitude review of the previous book was in terms of focus. Research has concentrated almost solely on attitudes to individual languages. Thus there is, for example, research on attitude to French (in Canada), attitude to Welsh, attitude to Gaelic (in Scotland), attitude to Irish and attitude to English. Occasionally, an attitude to a specified minority language is inappropriately referred to as attitude to bilingualism. It is the contention of a chapter in this book that attitude to bilingualism is different and conceptually distinct from attitude to a specific language. Attitude to bilingualism has two possible foci. In one sense, it is about two languages in contact. The relationship between two (or more) languages within a variety of contexts or domains can be explored in terms of individual attitudes. In a second sense, attitude to bilingualism is about a holistic, integrated version of bilingualism. As different from a fractional, decomposed, separatist attitude to two languages, another view of attitude to bilingualism may explore varieties of attitude to 'balanced', organic bilingualism. There is a danger of expressing an ideology when writing about attitude to bilingualism. Something organic, holistic and integrated seems preferable to that fractional, decomposed and separatist. The very language seems to leak a value system. It cannot be claimed that any approach, be it statistical, theoretical, methodological or psychological, is value free. Choices and decisions are continually made in writing and research, such that ideology is always latently present. However, the ideal of objectivity, the aim of a multi-sided viewpoint and being universally critical has been attempted in the reviews and research of this book.

The fifth and final deficiency noticed in reviewing research on language attitudes was the dominance of interest in attitude as part of an explanation of (second) language attainment or performance. The excellent research tradition stemming from Gardner & Lambert (1972), reviewed in Gardner (1985a), has culminated in Gardner's socio-educational model. In this model, attitude is one variable among others in the prediction of bilingual proficiency and non-linguistic outcomes (e.g. self concept, cultural values and beliefs). Attitude is regarded in this model as an input and an outcome as is illustrated in Figure P.1.

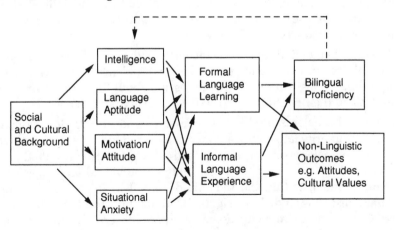

Figure P.1

The prediction of language proficiency by using attitudes to language is obviously important. The deficiency seems in the origins of language attitudes and attitude to bilingualism. Previous research has provided clues in bivariate relationships. For example, the type of school attended, language background and age may affect language attitudes. This book seeks, by a piece of research in Wales, to attempt to predict language attitudes by investigating their possible origins in individual variables, (e.g. age, gender, ability) and in contextual/environmental attributes (e.g. type of school attended, youth culture, language background). The relative effects of these attributes are examined in an overall model. Whereas much previous research asks 'What effects do attitudes have?' this book focuses on 'What factors create different attitudes?' and on 'What factors make attitude become more and less favourable over the crucial teenage years?'

Plan of the Book

The book does not attempt to make a comprehensive review of the various writings and research on attitudes and bilingualism. R.C. Gardner's (1985a) *Social Psychology and Second Language Learning: The Role of Attitudes and Motivation* and Baker's (1988) *Key Issues in Bilingualism and Bilingual Education* may be consulted for such a review. Rather the book seeks to highlight some key substantive issues in research on attitudes and bilingualism, and attempts to advance both thinking and research in this area.

The arrangement of the book is in terms of a dualism. Substantive issues emanating from theory and research are followed by research illustrating and advancing those issues. The content of the substantive issues chapters will now be introduced.

The first chapter defines the wider context of the book. Consideration is given to the nature of attitudes, particularly to problems in specifying what is an attitude. This is followed by discussion about the measurement of attitudes and their relationship to action and everyday behaviour.

Some of the major issues located by research into attitudes to language, especially minority languages, are then considered in the second chapter. A critique of major issues in language attitudes suggests that such theory and research has concentrated on attitude to individual languages (e.g. attitude to French (in Canada) and attitude to Welsh). In contrast, attitude to bilingualism has tended to be ignored. Studies on attitude to a minority language sometimes implicitly assume they are concerned with bilingualism. It is sometimes assumed that attitude to the Welsh language is the same as, or an indicator of, attitude to bilingualism. The fourth chapter attempts to argue for, and illustrate, a holistic, integrated, harmonic view of bilingualism as opposed to a fractional, separatist, decomposed approach. Within this framework, attitude to bilingualism becomes different and distinct from attitude to a language.

The fifth chapter highlights a crucial issue that seems latent and not formally addressed in writings and discussions on language policy and planning. Where languages are in danger of decline or extinction, or when cultures and languages are overtly being conserved by, for example, educational policies, changing attitudes is often prominently on the agenda. It is usually accepted that whatever the language policy, planning or provision, the favourability or unfavourability of attitudes in the population fundamentally affects the success or otherwise of language preservation. Thus changing attitudes is often a major part of the formal or hidden agenda of language planning. The fifth chapter therefore draws out important issues in the theory and research of attitude change relevant to language policy and planning.

Following the substantive chapters, research chapters attempt to illustrate and extend those substantive issues. Chapter 3 examines the relationship between important personal and environmental variables and attitude. The relative effect of language environment, youth culture, nature of school and individual characteristics is examined in terms of their relationship to language attitudes.

Attitude to bilingualism as a measurable construct is explored in Chapter 4. Whether attitude to bilingualism is distinct from attitude to a language is tested and found clearly definable. Its relationship to individual differences and environmental variables is then explored. A model of attitude to bilingualism is constructed by structural equation modelling.

Chapter 6 examines attitude change amongst a large sample of secondary (high) school pupils. The assumption is that the teenage years comprise one crucial era in the evolution of attitude to a minority language and attitude to bilingualism. An attempt is made to elucidate reasons for such attitude change by a variety of personal and contextual attributes. The relative power of such variables provides feedback into a discussion about attitude change and language planning. The book concludes by returning to the issues and aims expressed in this introduction.

The research related in this book was financed by a grant from the Economic and Social Research Council and was undertaken between 1988 and 1990. The research draws its sample from Wales. In the Welsh context, a wide variety of aspects of bilingual societies are present. Welsh is a minority language spoken by close to one in five of the population. However, there are areas of Wales (e.g. parts of the county of Gwynedd) where Welsh is spoken by high proportions (50% to 90%) of the residents (Baker,

1985). Welsh is the indigenous language with the topic of immigration vigorously debated. The minority language is threatened by the inward movement of the English language and monolingualism. Issues regarding the preservation of the minority language, bilingual education, language rights, language planning, multiculturalism, integration and assimilation are all encapsulated in the Welsh context. Simply, the Welsh context provides a rich research ground. While naive generalisation from the Welsh context to other countries and contexts is an activity fraught with danger, the Welsh situation is a rich microcosm of minority language problems, practices and potentialities.

To keep as many readers as possible interested in the research chapters, such chapters have been written with the non-statistical reader in mind. An attempt has been made to minimise the amount of technical information in these three chapters and provide a more literary account. Where there are numerical results and tables, most should be understandable at an intuitive level. At the same time, it is important and necessary to provide full details of the methodological and statistical approaches taken. This allows the assumptions of the research to be made explicit. In a detailed Appendix, the approaches taken to both techniques of data collection and to statistical analysis are outlined and discussed. The intention is to reveal overtly some of the decision making process that is too often hidden in research. This appendix also contains more technical details of the analysis.

To summarise. The overall aim of the book is to break new ground by attempting to:

(1) Establish attitudes as more central in research on bilingualism and languages.
(2) Ensure language attitudes theory and research is informed by the strong tradition of attitude theory and research from social psychology.
(3) Establish the considerable relevance of attitude change theory to language restoration and decay. Language policy and planning can be informed by insights from the social psychology of attitude change.
(4) Illustrate how language attitude research can use recent developments in psychometric measurement and model building to enhance sophistication in measurement, power in analysis and increase understanding of language attitudes.
(5) Establish, at a conceptual and operational level, attitude to bilingualism as distinct from attitude to a language.
(6) Examine the origins of attitude to a language and attitude to bilingualism in terms of individual and contextual variables.

The aim is therefore to place attitudes higher up the menu in bilingual philosophy, policy, planning, provision and practice. The aim is also to show that the ingredients of attitudes are helpfully defined from within social psychological theory and research. At the end of the meal, it is hoped that an appetite will be gained to refine and improve the recipe. The book seeks to suggest some new and improved tastes with the hope that some will gain, while others will extend and improve.

1 Attitudes and Language: Foundational Issues

Introduction

There are two overlapping aims to this chapter. The first aim is to explore the nature, meaning and importance of the term 'attitude'. Second, the aim is to ensure that later discussion of language attitudes is refined and informed by reference to the well established body of literature in social psychology on attitude theory, attitude research and attitude change. The tendency of research on language attitudes (the Welsh research is an example) is to appear to ignore or be unaware of the strong tradition in social psychology that concerns the definition, structure and measurement of attitudes, the relationship of attitudes to external behaviour and the central topic of attitude change. Much language attitudes research (see Gardner, 1985a; Baker, 1988) has tended to be atheoretical and piecemeal in evolution. There is typically little or no reference to attitude theory, little or no awareness of changes and refinements in attitude theory and research that have occurred in the last six decades. Measurement of attitude has sometimes ignored the problems of single item measurement, failed to establish the reliability of scales (especially internal consistency), and not investigated whether the scales are unidimensional or multidimensional. Small unrepresentative samples and simple bivariate statistical relationships tend to be used in such research. There are exceptions. The sampling procedure of Sharp et al. (1973), the variety of attitude scaling devices (Sharp et al., 1973) and the concern for reliability and dimensionality of Gardner (1985a, 1985b) are examples of good practice.

This chapter seeks to locate language attitude research firmly within its parent discipline—the social psychology of attitudes. It is the contention of this chapter that unless such a foundational perspective is taken, discussions and research about attitudes and languages are likely to be naive, not well defined, prone to replicate previous mistakes and in danger of re-inventing the wheel. The applied nature of much language attitudes research may mean the focus of such research is different from that of pure attitude theorists. Nevertheless, just as a mechanic building his or her own special car is best informed by the general theory of car mechanics, the language attitude scholar can valuably be informed by attitude theory.

The Importance of Attitudes

Whether it be a new student of bilingualism or a novitiate into sociology, education or psychology, the jargon within a discipline may appear both frightening and immense. Terminology within each of these disciplines teems like torrential rain. There is, therefore, a need to defend the term attitude as a valuable concept within the study of bilingualism.

There are a number of reasons why attitude is a central explanatory variable. Three reasons will be highlighted. First, the term appears to be part of the terminology system of many individuals. That is, it is not a jargon word invented by specialised psychologists that has narrow utility within a small group of people. Attitude is a term in common usage. While social psychologists may wish to give a more highly defined meaning to attitude, there appears to be sufficient overlap in the use of the term between social psychologists and the public to allow chains of inter-communication. Common terminology allows bridges to be made between research and practice, theory and policy. Common terminology also reduces the tendency to scientism (Harre *et al.*, 1985)—the replacement of common terms by scientific jargon.

In ordinary conversation we speak of the importance of attitudes in the restoration of health. A positive attitude to healthy eating and exercise may increase life expectancy. In the life of a language, attitudes to that language appear to be important in language restoration, preservation, decay or death. If a community is grossly unfavourable to bilingual education or the imposition of a 'common' national language is attempted, language policy implementation is unlikely to be successful.

This illustration provides a second reason why attitude is an important concept. A survey of attitudes provides an indicator of current community thoughts and beliefs, preferences and desires. Attitude surveys provide social indicators of changing beliefs and the chances of success in policy implementation. In terms of minority languages, attitudes, like Censuses, provide a measure of the health of the language. A survey of attitude to French in Canada, attitude to Spanish in the USA, attitude to English in Japan might reveal the possibilities and problems of second languages within each country. As E.G. Lewis (1981) observed:

> Any policy for language, especially in the system of education, has to take account of the attitude of those likely to be affected. In the long run, no policy will succeed which does not do one of three things: conform to the expressed attitudes of those involved; persuade those

who express negative attitudes about the rightness of the policy; or seek to remove the causes of the disagreement. In any case knowledge about attitudes is fundamental to the formulation of a policy as well as to success in its implementation (p. 262).

The status, value and importance of a language is most often and mostly easily (though imperfectly) measured by attitudes to that language. Such attitudes may be measured at an individual level, or the common attitudes of a group or community may be elicited. At either level, the information may be important in attempting to represent democratically the 'views of the people'. However, attitudes do not just provide opinion polls. As Marsh (1982) argues, 'The key to the correct use of survey data to provide corroborative evidence of a causal process is in the adoption of a model (p. 72). That is, a survey may aid understanding of social processes. Consideration of how attitudes relate to their causes and effects may provide insights into human functioning.

The third reason why attitude is an important concept lies in its continued and proven utility. That is, within education and psychology, it has stood the tests of time, theory and taste. From the early days of Charles Darwin (1872), Thomas & Znaniecki (1918) and Thurstone & Chave (1929), the modern psychological conception of attitude has been described as 'one of the key concepts of social psychology or even as the most distinctive and indispensable concept in (American) social psychology' (Jaspars, 1978: 256). Specification of the modern conceptualisation of attitude is left to the next section. For the moment, the suggestion is that, for over sixty years, attitude has repeatedly proven a valuable construct in theory and research, policy and practice. Topics from religion to race, sport to sex, languages to LSD have used attitudes as an important explanatory variable.

Three reasons for the importance of attitude have been highlighted. Its close connection to individual construct systems, its value as an indicator of viewpoints in the community and its centrality in psychological theory and research for over sixty years attest to attitude as a central topic. Such a justification, however, demands a more detailed explication of 'attitude'.

The Nature of an Attitude

Attitude is a hypothetical construct used to explain the direction and persistence of human behaviour. We all explain behaviour by reference to relatively stable and enduring dispositions in people. Those who spend time by themselves and shun gregariousness may be called shy. Someone who believes in prayer and dislikes profanities may be said to have a favourable attitude to religion. Clearly an attitude to something is not like height, weight or attending church. Height, weight and church attendance can be directly observed and accurately measured. In comparison, attitudes cannot be directly observed. A person's thoughts, processing system and feelings are hidden. Therefore attitudes are latent, inferred from the direction and persistence of external behaviour. Attitudes are a convenient and efficient way of explaining consistent patterns in behaviour. Attitudes often manage to summarise, explain and predict behaviour. Knowing someone's attitude to alcohol, for example, may sum up likely behaviour in a range of contexts over time.

The original use of the term attitude embodied something different from its current meaning. Attitude originally meant a posture or pose in painting or drama, as in 'adopt an attitude of innocence'. Derived from the Latin word 'aptitude' and the Italian 'atto' (Latin = *actus*), its root meaning, however, appears to be 'aptitude for action'. That is, having a tendency towards certain actions. This is embodied in Allport's (1935) classic definition. For Allport, attitude is 'a mental or neural state of readiness, organized through experience, exerting a directive or dynamic influence upon the individual's response to all objects and situations with which it is related'. A variety of definitions of attitude exist (Jahoda & Warren, 1966; Jaspars, 1978; Shaw & Wright, 1967). These definitions vary from the stipulative, operational and metatheoretical to the mathematical.

Definitions of attitude are surrounded by semantic disagreements and differences about the generality and specificity of the term. The working definitions preferred here are by Ajzen (1988) and McGuire (1985). For Ajzen (1988), an attitude is 'a disposition to respond favourably or unfavourably to an object, person, institution, or event', (p. 4). For McGuire (1985), attitudes locate objects of thought on dimensions of judgement. An example would be a language as an object being seen as favourable or unfavourable. As will be seen later, this definition links with attitude measurement (e.g. favourable or unfavourable attitudes to the Welsh language or bilingualism). Also, the specification of objects, persons, institutions or events is important and valuable in constructing measurement scales.

For Bem (1968), attitudes are self descriptions or self perceptions. In this perspective, individuals come to recognise their attitudes by observations of their own behaviour. People observe themselves speaking French, for example. Consequently they infer that they must possess a favourable attitude to French. Thus language attitudes may be constructed through inspection of one's own actions. This is regarded by Bem (1972) as parallel to inferring the attitude of other people by observing their behaviour.

Attitude As Input and Output

Further explication of attitude comes from educational research, where attitude is considered both as input and output. For example, a favourable attitude to maths or to language learning may be a vital input in maths or language achievement. In this sense, attitude is a predisposing factor, affecting the outcomes of education. Attitude can also be an outcome in itself. After a reading programme or a language learning course, the teacher may hope for a favourable attitude to reading or the language learnt. Sometimes attitude may be as important an outcome as achievement if further development or interest in a subject is sought. A skilled reader may shun books after formal education. A less skilled reader with a love of books may, because of a favourable attitude, carry on reading regularly into adulthood. Thus attitude serves a double function. It is an important concept as it provides a presage and a product variable, a predisposer and an outcome. In Gardner's (1983, 1985a) socio-educational model, attitude is placed alongside intelligence, aptitude and anxiety as an initial ingredient in bilingual proficiency. Language attitudes also appear in the model as an outcome alongside bilingual proficiency.

The Three Components of Attitude

A classical explication of attitude is to follow Plato and distinguish between the cognitive, affective and readiness for action parts of attitudes. The cognitive component concerns thoughts and beliefs. A favourable attitude to the Irish language might entail a stated belief in the importance of continuity of the indigenous language, its value in the transmission of Irish culture and use in immersion bilingual education. The affective component concerns feelings towards the attitude object (e.g. the Irish language). The feeling may concern love or hate of the language, a passion for Irish poetry, or an anxiety about learning a minority language.

The cognitive and affective components of attitude may not always be in harmony. A person may express favourable attitudes to Irish language education. More covertly, that same person may have negative feelings about such education. Irrational prejudices, deep-seated anxieties and fears may occasionally be at variance with formally stated beliefs. In attitude measurement, formal statements are made reflecting the cognitive component of attitudes. These may only reflect surface evaluations. Doubt has to be expressed whether deep-seated, private feelings, especially when incongruent with preferred public statements, are truly elicited in attitude measurement. Such measurement may not always delve beneath the surface. Overtly stated attitudes may hide covert beliefs. Defence mechanisms and social desirability response sets tend to come inbetween stated and more secret attitudes.

The action or conative component of attitudes concerns a readiness for action. It is a behavioural intention or plan of action under defined contexts and circumstances. A person with a favourable attitude to Irish might state they would send their children to a bilingual school. A person with a favourable attitude to bilingualism might indicate their readiness to enter adult language classes. This latter example illustrates the possibility of the action component often, but not always being an indicator of external behaviour. However, as will be considered later, the relationship between attitudes and action is neither straightforward nor simple.

This three component model of attitude is best viewed in a hierarchical form (Rosenberg & Hovland, 1960) with cognition, affect and action as the foundation. These three components merge into a single construct of attitude at a higher level of abstraction (Ajzen, 1988; Rosenberg & Hovland, 1960; Ajzen & Fishbein, 1980), as illustrated in Figure 1.1.

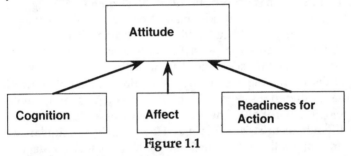

Figure 1.1

Ajzen (1988) summarises this pattern:

The hierarchical model of attitude, then, offers the following account of the way in which attitudes affect behaviour. The actual or symbolic presence of an object elicits a generally favourable or unfavourable evaluative reaction, the attitude towards the object. This attitude, in turn, predisposes cognitive, affective, and conative responses to the object, responses whose evaluative tone is consistent with the overall attitude. (pp. 22, 23)

Attitude and Related Terms

Before moving on to examine how attitudes relate to external behaviour, a brief word is necessary about attitude and related terms such as ideology, motive and trait. Alongside attitude are close neighbour terms such as belief, concept, construct and opinion. It is possible to make subtle distinctions between attitude and related terms (e.g. see Shaw & Wright, 1967).

First, opinion can be defined as an overt belief without an affective reaction. In comparison, attitudes contain affective reactions. Second, opinions are verbalisable while attitudes may be latent, conveyed by non-verbal and verbal processes. Third, opinion surveys and attitude surveys differ. Opinion surveys tend to locate community or group preferences and wishes. Opinion polls provide indicators of population viewpoints. Attitude surveys focus more on the relationship of attitudes to a variety of other variables, seeking to understand human functioning. However, while tight distinctions aid precision and may avoid ambiguity within the confines of social psychology, everyday language usage does not tend to make such distinctions. Opinions and attitudes tend to be synonymous in everyday speech.

Within the field of language attitudes, the terms attitude and motive often appear without discussion of the extent of over-lap and difference (an exception is Gardner, 1985a). Both attitudes and motives refer to latent dispositions affecting the directionality of behaviour, but not to external behaviour itself (Shaw & Wright, 1967). Newcomb (1950) suggests a two-fold difference between attitude and motive. First, motives have an existing drive state, attitudes do not, although attitudes may produce drives. Second, attitudes are object specific, motives are goal specific. Whether these are merely fine semantic discriminations or real distinctions for which a discriminating terminology is required, is a moot point. The more important difference seems to lie in the terms representing two different psychological traditions. The two traditions of attitude and motivation have different theorists and disciples. However, there is similarity between the terms, especially when reified into contexts such as language problems and language planning. As McGuire (1985) states 'Distinctions deserve to be made only insofar as they make a difference such that the distinguished variables relate differently to third variables of interest' (p. 241).

The use of the terms 'attitude' and 'motivation' has varied within the areas of bilingualism and second language acquisition. Schumann (1978), Brown (1981) and Gardner (1985a) use the terms in different ways from each other and sometimes differently from their theoretical construction in social psychology. Ellis (1985) discusses the use of attitude and motivation by these authors and concludes that 'there is no general agreement about what precisely "motivation" or "attitudes" consists of, nor of the relationship between the two. This is entirely understandable given the abstractness of these concepts, but it makes it difficult to compare theoretical propositions' (p. 117).

The difference between ideology and attitude is also partly about different traditions of research, theory and expression, particularly between sociology and social psychology. Cooper & McGaugh (1966) regard ideology as an elaborate cognitive system rationalising forms of behaviour (e.g. 'political' behaviour at whatever level). Ideology tends to refer to codifications of group norms and values. At an individual level, ideology tends to refer to broad perspectives on society—a philosophy of life. In this sense, ideology may be a global attitude. A psychological approach to attitude will tend to acknowledge both the group and individual representations of attitude (perhaps with more accent on the individual). However attitudes tend to be specific to objects (e.g. attitude to the Frisian language). The relationship between attitude and ideology is further explored by McGuire (1985).

Finally, the difference between attitude and personality trait is worth stating. Attitudes and personality traits (e.g. extroversion) are both assumed to be relatively stable, enduring hypothetical dispositions which manifest themselves in observable behaviour. Attitudes tend to be thought of as comparatively more open to change and modification. This is particularly because attitudes are evaluative of objects or people. Personality attributes are not typically conceived of as involving an evaluative process. Personality traits do not have a target whereas attitudes are directed towards a target (Ajzen, 1988). Both terms are used to explain behaviour, but are often distinct both in psychological theory and in human discourse.

Attitudes and Behaviour

In the 1960s, there developed criticisms of attitudes regarding their role and utility in predicting and explaining human behaviour (e.g. Wicker, 1969; McGuire, 1969). The first criticism was that comparison of seemingly related actions revealed little consistency between such actions. People may be polite in one situation, rude in the next. People may say they are ambitious in one context, purport to be unambitious in a different context. The most famous instance is LaPiere's research (1934) where a Chinese couple were refused service in only one of 251 restaurants in the USA. A letter sent to these same restaurants six months later revealed that 92% of establishments said they would refuse entry to a Chinese couple. Actual behaviour was seemingly incongruent with expressed attitudes.

This does not mean that observation of external behaviour leads to accurate and valid understanding while expressed attitudes deceive. Such a conclusion is too often and too hastily reached. Observation of external behaviour may produce mis-categorisation and wrongful explanation. Such behaviour may be consciously or unconsciously designed to disguise or conceal inner attitudes. A person may appear overtly friendly and interested in Gaelic speaking Scots. The inner attitude may be disdainful and arrogant. A direct, predictive relationship between attitude and external behaviour can no more be assumed than that between behaviour and attitude. The psychologists ability to predict action from attitude, or attitude from action, is somewhat imperfect. Behaviour tends not always to be consistent across contexts. As props on the stage change, as different actors and actresses change, different scripts are enacted, and repertoires of behaviour are available or not, behaviour may change accordingly, and attitudes may become imperfect explainers and predictors of behaviour. As Ajzen (1988) argues, 'Every particular instance of human action is, in this way, determined by a unique set of factors. Any change in circumstances, be it ever so slight, might produce a different reaction' (p. 45).

In the last two decades, the criticisms of the 1960s regarding the value of attitude as a psychological construct have given way to a more sophisticated and better defined conception of attitude. First, to ignore the accumulated experiences that are captured in attitudes and concentrate solely on external behaviour is unjustified. Acts of external behaviour are themselves the result of a particular and complex environment. To understand why someone attends an eisteddfod (Welsh cultural festival) may require reference to a large variety of personal, interpersonal and situational factors. General response patterns and relatively stable dispositions are not necessarily easily inferred from single acts of behaviour or from an interview with a person. This argument moves to a current belief that underlying attitudes can be indicated by observation of behaviour or, more efficiently, by *self reports*. Both observation and self reports can validly (and sometimes invalidly) indicate latent response dispositions. Further, attitudes may be better predictors of future behaviour than observation of current behaviour. Attitudes tend to be less affected by situation factors, and can be measured more reliably.

Second, a key element in attitude measurement is the *generality or specificity* of the attitude in question. Attitude to minority languages, attitude to the Irish language, attitude to praying in Irish in church on Sunday represents three levels of generality. Defined acts also vary in their generality (e.g. from inter-relationships with Irish speakers in general, to speaking Irish on Saturday nights in a public house with defined neighbours). Predictive validity is enhanced when the level of generality is the same, and decreased when different levels are being used. For example, inferring a disposition to spend a holiday in the Gaeltacht from attitude to the Irish language moves between two different levels of generality and invites only a small relationship. Attitude to Irish is more compatible with a more aggregated response tendency.

It has already been suggested that there can be a lack of consistency in single actions on different occasions due to the presence of unique factors. However, *aggregation across occasions* provides a relatively stable measure of the likelihood of the performance of behaviour within a band of generality. Broad response patterns (and not specific behaviours) are mostly satisfactorily indicated from attitude measures. Broad attitudes are poor predictors of very specific actions. Human behaviour is mostly consistent, patterned and congruent in terms of attitudes and action, so long as the same levels of generality are used.

Via concern for reliable and valid measurement, the use of mediational and contextual variables, appropriate aggregation across a variety of tendencies and establishing the generality level at which one is working, the pessimism about attitude research in the 1960s has given way to attitudes being re-established as important to human understanding in the 1990s. However, the use of attitude as a research variable also depends on satisfactory measurement devices. The attitude–action relationship can be enhanced by greater concern for reliability and validity in attitude measurement. Using multiple items (e.g. a Likert scale) rather than a single item usually enhances internal reliability. Similarly, ensuring a scale is unidimensional and not confusing two or more entities, aids the attitude–action relationship. It is to such measurement of attitudes this chapter now turns.

The Measurement of Attitudes

A variety of alternative methods exist for measuring an individual's attitude: Thurstone & Chave (1929), Likert (1932), Guttman's Scalogram analysis, the Semantic Differential Technique, the Repertory Grid Technique, Factor Analysis and Sociometry being varied examples. Document analysis, content analysis, interviews, case studies, autobiographies and the matched guise technique are also well established alternatives. The specific attitude under investigation may include attitudes to language groups (e.g. Welsh speakers), a language itself, its features, uses, cultural associations, learning a language, bilingual education as product or process, language preference, policy and practice (Giles, Hewstone & Ball, 1983).

One of the most popular methods of attitude measurement is to produce an attitude scale composed of statements such as:

Welsh people speak too much English

Welsh should not be forced on non-Welsh pupils.

Responses may be Agree/Disagree or be measured more exactly with a five point scale:

| *Strongly Agree* | *Agree* | *Neither Agree nor Disagree* | *Disagree* | *Strongly Disagree* |

Summation of scores on various statements may finally produce one score per respondent, or, if factor analysis is used, several scores on sub-scales. Most measurement techniques force an attitude into unidimensional structure, resulting in one score on a general scale. Factor analysis allows multidimensionality. Attitude to Welsh, for example, may better be broken down into components (e.g. attitude to the language; attitude to Welsh speaking people; attitude to the functional or instrumental use of Welsh).

The Semantic Differential Technique is less popular but may sometimes tap the affective component as well as the cognitive component of attitudes. A good example is to be found in Sharp *et al.* (1973). Meanings attached to a stimulus (The Welsh Language) can be profiled for an individual, or when calculated as an average, for a group, as shown for example, in Figure 1.2.

Unmusical				*	Musical
Ugly			*		Beautiful
Difficult	*				Easy
Old Fashioned		*			Modern
Useless				*	Useful
Weak			*		Strong

Figure 1.2

Figure 1.2 is a hypothetical profile of a group and suggests the Welsh language is seen as relatively Musical, Difficult, Old Fashioned and Warm. Certain pairs of bi-polar adjectives may mostly represent the cognitive aspects of attitude (e.g. Useless–Useful); other pairs may tap feelings regarding meanings (Cold–Warm). Profiles of different groups may be compared as well as individuals contrasted.

The measurement of an individual's attitudes is unlikely to reveal their attitudes perfectly. There are a number of reasons why attitude measurement is rarely, if ever, totally valid (see Potter & Wetherall (1987) for a radical critique). Three of the more prominent problems are listed below:

(1) People may respond to an attitude test in a way that makes them appear more prestigious, more good than is real. Consciously and unconsciously people tend to give socially desirable answers, and put themselves in the best light (halo effect). A person may wish to be seen as pro-Welsh language, even if the private attitude is something different.

(2) People may be affected in their response to an attitude test by the researcher and the perceived purpose of the research. The ethnic identity, gender, status, age, language in its verbal and non-verbal forms, and the social class of the researcher may each affect how an individual responds to an attitude test. The perceived aim and objective of the research (e.g. in support of minority languages or anti-immigration) may similarly affect replies, as may the context or environment of the testing.

(3) A good attitude test needs to encompass the full range of issues and ideas involved in a topic. The initial item pool must cover the fullest range of possible attitudes in terms of topic, complexity and favourability and unfavourability. An item analysis on the item pool (to exclude the more unreliable items) must be executed on a representative and not atypical sample of people.

The measurement of attitudes is unlikely to warrant one style of approach. Whether the matched guise technique is chosen, for example, or Likert scaling, depends on the topic of research and preference in methodology (e.g. for an experiment or multivariate psychometric surveys). One recent movement has been towards adopting a systems style. This style includes an inclusive research design in terms of multiple variables, in a multilevel context, looking for interactions between variables, multiple pathways of causality and bi-directional cause–effect links. This style is illustrated in the research chapters of this book. Part of the systems approach is avoiding the extremes of narrow, pre-ordinate hypotheses and avoiding indiscriminate 'fishing' for statistically significant results. Exploring the data with descriptive statistics for the story it tells (rather than the story we want or expect it to tell) is joined by a reduction of variables by techniques such as factor (latent variable) analysis. A model of relationships between a reduced set of variables may then be postulated. Using, for example, structural equation techniques, the model may be tested, even discovered. A possible causal flow between the variables may be tested and refined.

As the following chapters will illustrate, research on language attitudes in the 1940s, 1950s and 1960s looked at single relationships (e.g. the link between age and the Welsh language; the relationship between language attitudes and language proficiency or performance). Gardner's (1985a) socio-educational model signalled a more complex, sophisticated, multivariate, causal approach. Attitudes become one element within an elaborate system of bilingual proficiency. One important part of this systems approach is to detect the relative importance of variables in the model. For example, is age or gender or language background or type of school attended more important in building a language attitude? What is the rank order of importance when direct causal effects and indirect effects, mediated through other variables, are combined (see Chapter 3)?

Another important part of a systems approach is the inclusion of contextual or environmental effects in addition to individual attributes. As important in a system as are individual differences (e.g. abilities, aptitudes, personality, motivation), the social nature of attitude formation and expression requires any explanation to include variation in social experience. Contexts such as language background, type of youth culture experienced, type of school attended affect attitudes. Reference to Ajzen & Fishbein's (1980) theory of reasoned action also points to the importance of behavioural intentions and social norms as part of a systems approach. Attitudes towards a specific behaviour may be a better predictor of intention and external behaviour than attitude to an object, although in language attitudes this is not always possible. A systems approach can also take in the mediation perspective (Cooper & Croyle, 1984). The dynamics of attitudes requires not only good measurement, but concern for personality factors (e.g. self-monitoring tendency) and situation factors that make for a stronger relationship between attitude and action.

Conclusions

This opening chapter has sought to show that attitudes are both central to the understanding of human behaviour and are capable of explication and measurement. Some would argue that attitudes are important because, over seven decades, there has developed a strong theoretical and research tradition on attitudes. Attitudes in social psychology have withstood tests of fashion and criticism, and maintained a central position. Simple relationships between attitudes and behaviour are no longer expected. When aggregation across time, context, people, when internal and external conditions and the level of specificity or generality are taken into account, attitude remains an important construct in the analysis of dispositional tendencies.

Another reason was given for the importance of attitudes. Given that attitudes can be adequately defined, theoretically explicated and reliably and validly measured, there appears another defence for the place of attitudes in the study of bilingualism. Attitude tends to be a natural part of the language of everyday discussion of language life. The administrator and not just the academic, the teacher and not just the theorist, the raconteur and not just the researcher tend to use the term attitude as part of everyday expression. Correspondence between scientific and everyday language can be a mixed blessing. Within bilingualism and minority language activity, it appears to be a blessing rather than a curse. Research on attitudes has a potentially improved chance of being applied. There is also the enhanced possibility of communication between theory and practice, research and reform, data and debate.

Attempting language shift by language planning, language policy making and the provision of human and material resources can all come to nothing if attitudes are not favourable to change. Language engineering can flourish or fail according to the attitudes of the community. Having a favourable attitude to the subject of language attitudes becomes important in bilingual policy and practice.

2 The Origin of Language Attitudes

Introduction

The dominant theme of this chapter is the building of a model of language attitudes. In the first chapter it was suggested that one recent major approach to language attitudes requires increased care in measurement and increasing the number of variables in a more sophisticated, overall analysis. This chapter outlines the nature of that approach and considers the important parts that may need to be included in a systems model of the creation of language attitudes.

In constructing a systems model of language attitudes, the chapter focuses on possible origins of such attitudes. There have been other important focuses on language attitudes they are not the prime subject of this chapter. For example, the tradition started by Gardner & Lambert (1972) focuses on the role of attitudes and motivation in second language learning. The rationale of this research tradition (see Gardner, 1985a) is to capture the major variables that make for language proficiency (e.g. intelligence, language aptitude, social and cultural background). These variables are then systematically arranged in a systems model.

Another example of important themes in language attitudes includes the experimental approach of the matched guise technique used to infer attitudes to language varieties (e.g. Welsh accented English, Welsh, English Received Pronunciation). Evaluations of speakers of particular languages or dialects provides an indirect measure of language attitude, especially in terms of status, prestige and social preferences. Edwards (1977), for example, found different evaluations of Galway, Cork, Cavan, Dublin and Donegal accents in Ireland. Differences were found on dimensions of competence, social attractiveness and personal integrity. Bourhis *et al.* (1973) found that bilingual speakers in Wales received positive evaluations from non-Welsh speakers and Welsh speakers alike. The matched guise approach to language attitudes is reviewed in Ryan & Giles (1982) and Giles, Hewstone & Ball (1983).

Language attitudes have also been examined in terms of language preference, reasons for learning a language, language teaching, language groups and communities, uses of language, classroom processes in language lessons and parent's language attitudes. These are reviewed in Gardner (1985a). Such attitudes tend to have been measured directly by a questionnaire or attitude scale. It is this methodological approach that will now be examined.

Evolving a Systems Model of Language Attitudes

The early research tradition can be generally characterised as follows:

(i) The creation of items to measure language attitude. For example, Jones (1949, 1950) used a 22 item scale to measure attitude to the Welsh language. Gardner & Lambert (1972) used four items to measure an instrumental attitude to learning French (e.g. I think [French] will some day be useful in getting a good job).

(ii) The calculation of an overall attitude score by simple summation across the items, although the Thurstone scaling technique allows a weighting system.

(iii) Attitude scores are related to other variables such as age, gender, language attainment. Such relationships tend to be independent of each other. For example, an analysis of the connection between age and attitude is separated from an analysis of gender and attitude.

(iv) Relatively small, unrepresentative samples were used. For example, Jones (1949,1950) used single schools from the Rhondda Valley in South Wales and from Cardiff.

Before discussing the problems with the above four stages, it is important to stress that, within its historical context, language attitude measurement and analysis was often sophisticated and advanced. Jones' (1949, 1950) use of Thurstone scaling techniques, Gardner & Lambert's (1972) use of factor analysis and Sharp et al.'s (1973) stratified sampling of schools throughout Wales are each illustrations of methodological approaches that some published research in the 1980s failed to emulate. It is too easy to criticise with the hindsight of the developments in research methodology and statistics of the last two decades, while failing to remember that certain language attitude research attained excellence in its era.

Developments in methods of test construction and statistical analysis point to the necessity of avoiding small samples, simple measures, simple scoring and simple analysis. Such developments suggest the following as one approach to the direct measurement of language attitudes.

(1) Research, irrespective of it being theoretical or applied, needs to start from a grounding in attitude theory and research in general, and in

relevant areas of language attitude research. The piecemeal development of language attitude theory and research tends to incorporate
re-inventing the wheel, and making errors of a technical and substantive nature.

(2) Research needs to use previously validated and reliable attitude scales
or construct attitude scales with concern to meet three criteria :

Internal reliability

The problem of using a single item to measure an attitude is the unknown likelihood of a response to that item being consistent across a short
period of time (e.g. six weeks). Using three or four items also tends to lead
to a lack of reliability. For example, the way a person answers the three or
four items may result in a low coefficient of internal consistency (e.g. using
Cronbach's alpha). Such measurement of internal consistency requires a
value of 0.8 or above on a scale ranging from 0 to 1.0 (Kline, 1986). Even
with the better researched attitude tests, such internal reliability is either
ignored (e.g. Ó Riagain & Ó Gliasain, 1984) or does not reach a value of 0.8
(e.g. the reliabilities of 0.13 to 0.77 of the instrumental attitude scale,
Gardner, 1985b). As Saris & Stronkhorst (1984) demonstrated, low reliability of a test can affect the results of the research in an influential manner.
When internal reliability is added to the analysis, patterns of relationships
may change. Also, test–retest reliability is often problematic as Gardner
(1985a) discusses. Attitude change over time is often expected—hence
test–retest measurement may measure change and not stability.

Validity

The central concern is whether the attitude scale measures what it says
it measures. This may be checked by critical examination of the content of
the items (content validity), by relating the scale to a variety of 'present'
variables (criterion-related validity), 'future' variables (predictive validity), and to variables within a well established theoretical formulation
(construct validity). Gardner (1985b) provides an illustration of the method
of attitude validity assessment using his scales.

Dimensionality

With the majority of language attitude scales in use, there has been no
test of whether one or more entities has been measured. For example, Jones'
(1949, 1950) 22 items scale may be measuring a single construct 'attitude to
the Welsh language'. Alternatively, it is possible that the scale has two or
three dimensions. As will be discussed later, research on language attitudes has tended to utilise two distinct dimensions, integrative and in-

strumental attitudes. To test for undimensionality or multidimensionality, a large initial pool of attitude items needs subjecting to an exploratory or confirmatory factor analysis. Such a procedure is illustrated in the language attitudes research of CILAR (1975) in Ireland, and research reported in the following chapter. Such a technique aims to reduce a large number of individual attitude items to a small number of underlying latent dimensions. Part of factor analysis procedure allows the computation of scores for each individual on the one or more located dimensions. This is generally much preferable to simple summation of scores across attitude items as in the Likert (1932) approach, since it weights items differentially and increases internal reliability.

Also, reliable and valid measurement needs to occur with other variables included in the research, as apart from attitude variables. It is the choice of the variables in language attitude research that is the next concern of this chapter.

There are two opposite dangers in choice of variables in language attitude research. First, there is the trap of specifying single relationships to be examined. For example, age and attitude, gender and attitude, achievement and attitude. This tends to over-simplify by not examining interactions and total relationships. Second, there is the trap of collecting data on as many variables as possible, knowing that somewhere there will be statistically significant relationships. Even the better-known research on language attitude tends to have long lists of variables with so many tables of results, that it may sometimes be difficult to see the wood for the trees.

Choice of variables may usefully be built around three concerns. First, it is helpful to ensure research is related to, and aware of previous theory. Guiding theories allow the evolution of generalisable statements across time and contexts, may avoid duplication of effort, and falling into traps or making the errors of previous research. Second, it is important to locate variables found by previous research to be potent in their relationship to language attitudes. If self esteem, for example, has repeatedly found to be unconnected to a specific language attitude, there is little point in adding it to the list of variables. Third, the choice of variables can be related to the demands of applied research. If a sponsor, for example, needs to know about different attitudes in different organisations, such variables (especially contextual variables) become important to specify.

The culmination of a choice of variables may suggest the following:

(1) The use of multiple variables and not just pairs of variables.
(2) Looking for interactions between variables. For example, gender and age by themselves may be unrelated to attitude to a specific language, but in combination be important. For example, in the hypothetical Table

2.1, males and females both have an average of 50, as do 14 year olds and 15 year olds. However, younger males and older females have distinctly higher scores than older males and younger females. An important interaction between gender and age occurs.

Table 2.1

	Male Mean	Female Mean	Overall Mean
14 year olds	60	40	50
15 year olds	40	60	50
Overall Mean	50	50	50

(3) Considering contextual, situational effects. Attitudes are formed, enacted and changed through the interplay of individual attributes and social situations. The advent of multilevel analysis, which considers the properties of individuals, groups of people (e.g. in classes, schools, districts), allows different units and levels to be analysed in the same design (Baker, 1990b; Goldstein, 1987).

(4) Considering multiple pathways in links between variables. A simple illustration is given in Figure 2.1, which moves from a simple set of relationships to a more complex process. This is examined in detail in following chapters.

(5) Considering bi-directional links between variables. For example, attitudes may both affect, and be affected by, ability. This is illustrated in

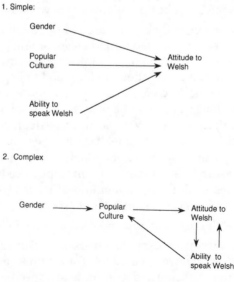

Figure 2.1

the second (complex) diagram above by the double arrow. In Chapter 1, it was suggested that (language) attitudes can be both an input and an output. In school, a favourable attitude to Spanish may both facilitate learning, and success in school may enhance attitude to a second or home language.

(6) Constructing a model of likely relationships between the multiple variables operationalised in the research. The 'complex' illustration above is a simple model specification with a small number of variables. Illustrative examples and further details may be found in Appendix 2.

Problems and Issues

That completes consideration of one suggested procedure in language attitudes research. Before moving to an examination of the variables located by previous research in language attitudes, some issues with the above approach need to be mentioned.

First, a choice of variables must be related to an awareness of the epistemological basis of the research methodology being adopted. In particular, the approach must be sensitive to the conflict between the hermeneutical, interpretive, phenomenological, verstehen paradigm in research methodology and the positivist, deterministic, mechanistic, scientific, objective, empirical paradigm. Each approach contains an implicit or explicit model of the social world. The approach implied in a systems model of language attitudes fits the scientific, objective ideal more favoured in psychology and often attacked by sociologists and anthropologists. A critique of this quantitative, scientific approach would include concern about artificial mechanisation, over simplification, over generalisation and isolation from the world as viewed by actors and actresses themselves. Alternative approaches would include those of ethnomethodologists, anthropologists and case study researchers. In such equally valuable and defensible styles of research, evidence of a wide variety is gathered rather than data on pre-ordinate variables. By interview and observation, explanations participants themselves provide (rather than scores on tests designed by the researcher), the resulting qualitative evidence becomes the basis for explanation and understanding. Understanding and explaining language attitudes can be undertaken by both an empirical and phenomenological perspective. Both paradigms provide insights and sagacity regarding language attitudes.

Second, the model needs to be based on an overt theory of language attitudes. Drawing on theory may avoid re-inventing the wheel, or making errors that have been previously exposed. It also means that research has the chance to become cumulative, coherent, generalisable and integrated. As Shipman (1981: 22-23) elucidates:

> Theories are essential ways in which social scientists make sense of their social world. They are attempts at a simplified model of that world. They are always influential because research, like any form of human interaction, is given meaning by those involved. All of us interpret our interactions with others to give them sense. Social scientists have accumulated a number of theoretical models of human behaviour. Each extends and simplifies available evidence. Conversely, these theoretical models will guide the selection of problems, procedures for collecting data,criteria for checking that the evidence is valid and ways of analysing and presenting results. The social scientist is qualified within a discipline that provides a number of such options for organising models of the social world................. being a functionalist or phenomenologist, behaviourist and so on, means that a specific system of organising perceptions about the social world has been adopted.

Third, the model proposed, tested and refined, requires replication across different samples, different populations, different contexts and across time. A model of language attitudes based on French Canadians in Quebec may not be replicated in Cardiff, Queensland or Catalonia. This is illustrated in Figure 2.2 which places the model in its wider context.

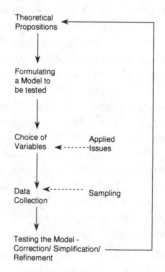

Figure 2.2

Fourth, the approach tends to assume an input-context-output design (see Baker 1985, 1988). Processes tend to be ignored. Systematic micro-analysis of classroom processes (e.g. Gliksman, 1976, 1981; Naiman *et al.*, 1978) tend to be missing from models. This accent on presage, context and product and exclusion of process, tends to make for a black box model of research. In such research the second by second interactions in the class-room are hidden from view. A process model, in comparison, tends to evoke a glass box model, where, for example, the classroom is open for viewing.

Fifth, finding a model which fits the data neither implies the model is correct, universal or unambiguously causal. The same dataset may be-queath several different models which fit the data. At its best, previous theoretical formulations and awareness of the problems of the dataset (e.g. measurement error) may guide the choice of the best fit model. At its worst, decisions may may be made from ideological preference, naivete or statis-tical significance rather than substantial significance. As Saris & Stronk-horst (1984) admit, despite the great advances made in causal modelling, no guarantees can be given that cause–effect relationships are present in the final model.

The Nature of Language Attitudes

The chapter now continues by discussing some of the key variables located by previous language attitude research that may need inclusion in a model of the origin of language attitudes. A delineation of key variables will depend on which aspect of language attitudes is being spotlighted. Language attitude is an umbrella term, under which resides a variety of specific attitudes. For example, research has variously focused on :

- attitude to language variation, dialect and speech style
- attitude to learning a new language
- attitude to a specific minority language (e.g. Irish)
- attitude to language groups, communities and minorities
- attitude to language lessons
- attitude to the uses of a specific language
- attitude of parents to language learning
- attitude to language preference

For the purposes of this chapter, one major area with a long tradition of research has been chosen. Attitudes to a specific language has a long history (cf. Jones 1949, 1950) and an international flavour, for example:

- attitude to Welsh (Jones, 1949, 1950; D. Sharp *et al.*, 1973; E. Glyn Lewis, 1975, 1981; Thomas & Williams, 1977; E. P. Jones 1982; Davies, 1980, 1986; see Baker, 1988 for a review)

• attitude to Gaelic (MacKinnon, 1981)
• attitude to Irish (CILAR, 1975; Ó Riagain & Ó Gliasain, 1984; see Fahy, 1988 for a review)
• attitude to French (e.g. Burstall et al., 1974; Gardner & Lambert, 1972; see Gardner, 1985a for a review of research)
• attitude to English (e.g. Sharp et al., 1973)
• attitude to Frisian (Smith, 1980)
• attitude to Asian languages (see Yatim (1988) and Au (1984) for reviews
• attitude to Norwegian (Svanes, 1987)

The interest in much of the research on attitudes to a specific language is on the reasons for favourability and unfavourability towards those languages. There is often a foundational interest in the valence of the attitude. As part of the 'market research' tradition in opinion surveys, a measure of language attitude may indicate the health of that language in society. The extent of goodwill may affect decisions of language policy and language planning. However, the more typical concern of research on attitudes to a specific language is on differences between groups of individuals. Thus differences according to gender, age or language background may be explored. Are females or males more favourably disposed to Gaelic? Are older people rather than younger people more favourable to Frisian in the Netherlands?

Unlike the research on the role of attitudes in attaining language competency (e.g. Gardner, Lalonde & Pierson, 1983), no model of attitude to a specific language has been advanced. Moving towards such a model is the task of the remainder of this chapter and is investigated by research in the following chapter. The first question in constructing a model is about attitude itself. As previously considered in this chapter, it is important to establish whether attitude to a particular language is unidimensional or multidimensional. For example, is attitude to Irish one unitary construct within the conceptualisation of respondents? Or does attitude to Irish in the 'minds' of those surveyed 'exist' in terms of a sub-structure or on a discrete number of dimensions?

Whether an attitude to a language has one general component or is multi-component in a hierarchical or multidimensional manner has received considerable research attention. The early research (e.g. Jones, 1949, 1950) assumed, a priori, that attitude to Welsh was one-dimensional. This is a particular, but avoidable, limitation with the Thurstone, Likert or Semantic Differential techniques of attitude measurement (see Baker, 1988). From Gardner & Lambert (1972) onwards, this one dimensional structure has been largely replaced. E. Glyn Lewis (1975), for example, makes a sixfold conceptual distinction between dimensions of attitude:

(1) General approval, e.g. 'I like speaking Welsh'.
(2) Commitment to Practice, e.g. 'I want to maintain Welsh to enable Wales to develop'.
(3) National Ethnic Tradition, e.g. 'We owe it to our forefathers to preserve Welsh'.
(4) Economic and Social Communication Importance, e.g. 'Welsh offers advantages in seeking good job opportunities'.
(5) Family and Local Considerations, e.g. 'Welsh is important in family life'.
(6) Personal, Ideological Consideration, e.g. 'Welsh provides a range of aesthetic experiences in literature'.

W.R. Jones (1966) also makes a conceptual distinction between four types of language attitude. First, there are attitudes which reflect an interest in a language. Jones (1966) suggested that this was the most important factor in learning Welsh. Second, there is the utilitarian attitude which Jones (1966) found became stronger as children approached school-leaving and careers. The remaining two types of attitude were attitude to the national character and attitude to proficiency in Welsh.

An *a priori* conceptual analysis of sub-dimensions is useful in gathering a comprehensive pool of items to measure attitude to a language. The problem with such conceptual distinctions is whether they are present within the personal constructions of individuals. Do people think along such dimensions? Are some dimensions missing from some or many people's attitude structures? Are some dimensions combined or even further distinguished internally? Therefore, some investigators have taken an *a posteriori* approach to the dimensionality of attitudes to a language. By using factor analysis, for example, the dimensions of attitude within a sample are explored. Such dimensions are hypothetical, latent constructs, but, when replicated across time, context and sample, aid the understanding of psychological processes in people.

Such replication of the dimensions of attitude to a language has occurred, although not without debate. Researchers across boundaries of time, sample and nation have located, in particular, attitude to language containing principally but not exclusively two parts: instrumental attitudes and integrative attitudes. The chapter now turns to a discussion of these two attitude components.

Instrumental and Integrative Attitudes

Two components of language attitudes have been located by research: an instrumental orientation and an integrative orientation. Instrumental motivation reflects pragmatic, utilitarian motives. It is characterised by 'a desire to gain social recognition or economic advantages through knowledge of a foreign language' (Gardner & Lambert, 1972: 14). Examples of instrumental items from Gardner (1985b) Attitude/Motivation Test Battery are as follows:

Studying French can be important to me because I think it will someday be useful in getting a good job.

Studying French can be important for me because it will make me a more knowledgeable person.

An instrumental attitude to a language is mostly self-oriented and individualistic and would seem to have conceptual overlap with the need for achievement (McClelland, 1958, 1961). Instrumental attitudes to learning a second language, or preserving a minority language might be, for example, for vocational reasons, status, achievement, personal success, self enhancement, self actualisation or basic security and survival.

An integrative attitude to a language, on the other hand, are mostly social and interpersonal in orientation. Such an attitude has conceptual links with the need for affiliation (Baker, 1976). It has been defined as 'a desire to be like representative members of the other language community' (Gardner & Lambert, 1972: 14). Examples of integrative test items are as follows (from Gardner, 1985b) :

Studying French can be important for me because it will allow me to meet and converse with more and varied people.

Studying French can be important for me because other people will respect me more if I have a knowledge of a foreign language.

Thus an integrative attitude to a particular language may concern attachment to, or identification with a language group and their cultural activities. Wanting to be identified with a defined group of 'other' language speakers, or wanting friendship within that group indicates an integrative orientation. The intensity of the implied interpersonal relationships may vary. At one end of the dimension may be gregariousness, with little attachment. At the other end of the dimension may be warm and close friendships. Somewhere in the middle comes sociability.

The casting of language attitudes under two headings, instrumental and integrative, is not without controversy (Oller, 1981; Au, 1984; Au, 1988). One strand of criticism concerns the tradition of measurement of the two orientations. From Gardner & Lambert (1959) to the present, the precise items to measure integrativeness and instrumentality have varied and often been small in number. In the most recent test battery (Gardner, 1985b), only four items measure each orientation. This tends to lead to low internal reliability. For example, Gardner, Lalonde & Moorcroft (1987) only found an alpha reliability coefficient of 0.55 for instrumentality (0.81 for integrativeness). A second strand of criticism is the varying use made of integrative and instrumental intentions. Sometimes they are kept distinct, other times aggregated. In the most recent test battery (Gardner, 1985b), a variety of individual scales are grouped into three categories: integrativeness, attitudes toward learning, and motivation. As Gardner (1988: 104) himself suggests, 'In some studies, scores on each measure are used as separate variables, in others the three composites are used, while in others a single aggregate is used. Which is used depends on the purpose of the study'.

The origin of the distinction between integrative and instrumental attitudes is conceptual rather than empirical. That is, an *a priori* distinction was made, which has a 'common-sense' appeal to it. Gardner & Smythe (1981) found that integrativeness is an identifiable factor when analysed alongside a wide variety of ability, achievement and general variables. Instrumentality did not emerge as a distinct entity. However, the specification of the variables put into the factor analysis directly affects the outcome. Were more 'instrumental' items present in the factor analysis, such a category of attitude may have been located. A further examination of this issue is found in the following chapter, where a piece of research directly address this problem.

Research into Integrative and Instrumental Attitudes

The major thrust of research using integrative and instrumental attitudes has been in their role in second language acquisition and achievement. The issue is the part attitudes play in second language learning. While aptitude for languages is one factor in the equation of why some learn quickly and others slowly, Gardner & Lambert's (1959) original study, found attitude as a second crucial factor. Attitude or motivation to learn a language was found to be independent of language aptitude. Students with higher ability or greater aptitude were not the only ones with favourable attitudes, nor were guaranteed to succeed in learning a second language. 'Those students who expended a considerable amount of energy in learning French as a second language were those who had favourable attitudes towards French-speaking people and who expressed an interest in learning French in order to get to know them better.' (Gardner, 1981: 103).

Furthermore, Gardner & Lambert (1959) concluded that 'the integratively oriented students are generally more successful in acquiring French than those who are instrumentally oriented' (p. 271). Gordon (1980) also found that people with integrative attitudes tended to have more favourable 'attitudes to second language learning than those with instrumental attitudes. However, there are certain reservations to be made. First, learning a second language and the act of becoming bilingual may invoke more favourable integrative attitudes (Strong, 1984). Integrative attitudes may both be the cause and effect of becoming or staying bilingual. The evidence suggests the most customary chronological order is integrative attitudes affecting learning (Gardner, 1985a). Second, people who score highly on the integrative dimension may not necessarily be motivated to learn a second language or maintain their bilingualism. Integrative attitudes may be directed at friendships, sociability or gregariousness without being focussed on language learning or maintenance. Third, some research has shown that attitudes other than an integrative one, promote the learning of a second language. Lukmani (1972) found that female school pupils in Bombay gave instrumental rather than integrative reasons for learning English. Gardner (1985a) notes two weaknesses in this conclusion: the measurement by Lukmani (1972) concerned orientation which is not precisely the same as motivation, and a lack of statistical significance in the comparison of orientations.

Fourth, the classification of reasons for learning a language into instrumental and integrative categories need not be straightforward (Oller, Hudson & Liu, 1977). For example, there is a difference between Burstall *et al.* (1974) and Lukmani (1972) who both include travelling abroad as an item in their measurement scales. The former authors regarded such travel as integrative, the latter author as instrumental. Factor analysis (e.g. Gardner & Smythe, 1975) does help a considerable amount in the clarification and classification of individual items on a scale. However, different groups of people from different contexts, different countries may validly interpret the same item in different ways. Travelling abroad, for example, could represent an integrative attitude for one person or ethnic group, an instrumental attitude for another person or group.

Fifth, these two orientations have been studied by research which concentrates on learning a second language. Little research exists on the way these attitudes explain the continuation of bilingual skills or the erosion of a language or bilingualism. The potential exists for language attitudes to become helpful explanatory variables in language decay where minority languages are declining or in peril. The lack of an integrative attitude with respect to relationships with, and amongst, the minority group may be a valuable concept at both the individual and societal levels of explanation. Similarly, lack of an instrumental attitude for economic, political, social, educational or vocational reasons may be a source of personal and group reasons for minority language decay. However, the power of these orientations in both minority language situations, especially where there is language erosion, has yet to be fully tested.

Sixth and finally, these two orientations are not necessarily opposites or alternatives. Both are capable of existing within an individual at the same time. A person may be motivated in different strengths by both orientations. It is possible to possess both instrumental and integrative attitudes, with different contexts and expectations affecting the balance of their relative power. Siguan & Mackey (1987) give the example of 'somebody who learns a language for the main purpose of becoming integrated in the group which speaks it may also believe that integration in the new group will have personal advantages for him and will even help him to rise in society' (p. 80).

Further Directions in Research

Since the seminal early study by Gardner & Lambert (1959), there has been a variety of research which examines the role of integrative and instrumental attitudes and motivation in language learning and the achievement of bilingualism. This is surveyed in detail by Gardner (1982, 1985a). Three important themes will be considered here.

Replication and consolidation

Since the early research, one focus has been on establishing the validity and power of the integrative attitude. Gardner (1985a) in a review of these studies concludes that the integrative attitude often, but not always, comes out of a factor analytical study as a separate, unitary variable. That is, there is some evidence to suggest that the motive is a well-defined and important component in explanations of language learning and bilingualism.

Another focus since the early research has found that the relationship between the integrative attitude and second language achievement is well replicated. Such an attitude does appear to be an important contributory factor in success in learning a second language. Yet as Gardner (1985a) and Oller, Hudson & Liu (1977) have pointed out, the degree of relationship between the integrative attitude and achievement in second language learning is small. Only about 5% of the variance in language achievement is usually accounted for by this motive. The percentage sounds small, but the variables accounting for achievement are likely to be many and complex. Allowing for error of measurement plus unaccounted variance due to variables not included in the research, 5% by tradition is small but definitely not negligible. The integrative attitude is one ingredient amongst many in the recipe for second language success.

Dissension and extension

A series of studies by Oller and his associates has seemingly found conflicting evidence to the tradition of research stemming from Robert Gardner and colleagues. Oller's research does not find a link between attitude and proficiency in a second language. Oller, Perkins & Murakami (1980), for example, found among students learning English as a second language in Southern Illinois that 'the degree of integrativeness of subjects is inconsistently related to scores on the language proficiency tests. In one case it appears to be negatively related' (p. 239). Oller, Hudson & Liu (1977) found that positive beliefs about a Chinese student's own cultural group rather than a target 'second language' group were the best predictors of second language proficiency. This research is complemented and contrasted by Genesee *et al.* (1983) who found that a student's expectation of motivational support from the target 'second language' group was a powerful predictor of second language proficiency. The research shows that attitudes do not exist within the individual in a vacuum. Intergroup factors provide one context where attitudes may be inhibited or promoted (Schumann, 1986).

Gardner (1985a) has attempted to reply to the findings of Oller and associates by pinpointing weaknesses in their type of research. Such limitations include invalidity and unreliability in measurement, different operational definition of motivations, using students from differing sources and creating one group which is not homogeneous, the nature of residualised predictors and the interpretation of beta coefficients in multiple regression analysis. On balance, the integrative attitude does seem a valuable variable in analysing second language achievement, but its relative effect must not be over-emphasised. Also, the integrative attitude must be viewed in a group and cultural context. Where a pupil is required or encouraged to learn a minority language (e.g. Welsh, Irish or Scottish Gaelic), cultural sanctions, perceived economic demands, religious affiliation and the target language group's expected reactions are all potentially important. That is, the presence of an integrative attitude may be kept latent if perceptions of reactions to the enactment of that attitude are negative. The best of intentions can be thwarted by the worst of conditions.

Attitudes and education

One theme relating language attitudes to education has been the factors contributing to language loss and language retention (Ramage, 1990). Thus Gardner, Lalonde & MacPherson (1985) found the favourable language attitudes was related to less attrition in a learnt language. Where learners had positive attitudes to a language they were less likely to lose competence in that language. Language attitude characteristics were also found to be a major factor in the retention of second language skills following an intensive language learning course (Gardner, Moorcroft & Metford, 1989).

Although the majority of the large number of researches on bilingualism and attitude would be regarded by their authors, at least, as having educational applications, the hope may too often be more pious than real. Much of the research gathers knowledge of psychological importance, without attempting to make direct observations about real educational practice. Indeed, much of the research, although using pupils and students, does not require the investigation to enter a school or a classroom. The research is essentially 'black-box'. The classroom realities are hidden from view. The research is of the input–output variety (Baker, 1985). The real life of the classroom, the process of motivation revealing itself in actual behaviour, is absent from most research on bilingualism and attitudes.

Two important studies preferred the 'glass box' tradition engaging motives as a central concept rather than attitudes. Here, the classroom is open for viewing. The real life drama of motive and language is studied. The process rather than presage and product are analysed. Thus Gliksman (1976, 1981) observed teenagers in school. In the first study observation was throughout the first term, and in the second study, 14-16 year olds were observed once every two weeks for four months. These pupils were classified by motivation tests as being integratively motivated or not. Gliksman (1976) hypothesised that the integrative motive influenced the type of participation of individuals in second language learning. Systematic observations were made of the number of times a pupil:

(i) volunteered information by raising a hand
(ii) was asked by teachers without volunteering
(iii) answered correctly or incorrectly
(iv) asked questions
(v) received positive, negative or no feedback from the teacher

In both the studies, integratively motivated students volunteered more frequently, gave more correct answers and received more positive reinforcement from the teacher than the non-integratively motivated students. The two groups did not differ significantly on the number of questions they asked in class. These relationships were not a primacy effect. They continued throughout the term, indicating consistent behavioural patterns.

In the second study, Gliksman (1981) also obtained ratings on a seven point scale of how interested the teenagers appeared during class. Integratively motivated pupils were rated as more interested in their lessons than the non-integratively motivated group, this being consistent over the whole term.

Naiman *et al.* (1978) also concentrated on pupil behaviour in class, differing from Gliksman (1981) in centring on the good language learner. The research issue was 'Do good learners tackle the language learning task differently from poor learners, and do learners have certain characteristics which predispose them to good or poor learning?' (p. 2) Seventy-two pupils aged 13-17 were observed, close to half of these pupils were 'good learners' and the remainder were among the less proficient. An integrative orientation was positively related to the number of times pupils volunteered to answer questions (r =0.37). An instrumental orientation was positively correlated to volunteering to answer questions (r =0.33) and inversely to giving incorrect responses (r = -0.23).

These two studies are important in showing that integrative and instrumental motivation are not just static variables measured like a snapshot by psychologists in abstraction of context. The studies show that in the classroom, motives enter the film of everyday life, a film that is dynamic and interactive.

Gardner's Socio-Educational Model

Gardner (1979, 1983, 1985a), having examined a variety of social psychological models of second language learning, presents his own more universal and empirically tested model. There are four stages to Gardner's model. First, the model begins with the social and cultural milieu. The child grows up in a community which transmits beliefs about language and culture. In many white communities in England, the transmitted belief is that bilingualism is unnecessary, difficult to achieve and, if achieved, it is at the expense of other areas of achievement. Such communities also tend to share the traditional United States philosophy of assimilation of minority cultures and languages. In some Canadian communities, opposite beliefs about French/English bilingualism and biculturalism exist, thus allowing the establishment, evolution and extension of bilingual schooling. The psychosocial influence of home, social group and type of language group (e.g. majority, minority) is further explored by Hamers & Blanc (1982, 1983, 1989) and Siguan & Mackey (1987).

The second stage of Gardner's (1979, 1983, 1985a) model is individual differences. This comprises four major variables; intelligence, language aptitude, motivation and situational anxiety. The child's social and cultural milieu affects individual differences which comprise four key individual variables. Attitudes and personality are not listed in this individual differences section, but are held to be subsumed in the four variables. This seems to confuse variables which may have negligible effects on language proficiency (e.g. personality traits) and concepts which have similarity and overlap (e.g. attitude and motives). (See Figure 2.3).

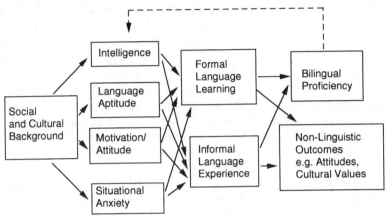

Figure 2.3 Gardner's socio-educational model (adapted from Gardner, 1985a)

Gardner (1985a) lists these four variables because 'intelligence is assumed to play a role because it determines how well or how quickly individuals understand the nature of any learning task or any explanations provided', (p. 147). Language aptitude concerns the degree of talent specific to learning any language; motivation concerns effort, desire and affect, and situational anxiety is viewed as important 'because it would have an inhibiting effect on the individual's performance, thus interfering with acquisition' (p. 148).

The third stage of Gardner's (1979, 1983, 1985a) model concerns the context where language is acquired. A distinction is made between formal and informal contexts of language acquisition. An example of a formal context is the classroom where a primary purpose is for pupils to learn to be linguistically competent and functionally bilingual. Drill and practice, audio-visual methods, translations and grammar exercises are examples of a formal, manifest and directed approach to language teaching. Informal contexts are where language learning is not the primary aim. Watching a French language film may be principally motivated by entertainment needs, and hence extending skills in French may be an unintended outcome. Talking to a friend or relative in Irish or Welsh may be for affiliative or social reasons. Practising skills and becoming more functionally competent may be a valuable incidental outcome but not a reason for such communication. However, formal and informal contexts may on occasions overlap. For example, talking to the teacher in the classroom at the end of a lesson, or listening to a radio programme for both learning and pleasure, are examples of where the formal merges with the informal.

Gardner (1985a) suggests that all four individual difference variables, intelligence, motivation, language aptitude and situational anxiety, influence the formal learning context. In informal contexts, motivation and situational anxiety are the principal determinants of entry into that context. Intelligence and language aptitude play a secondary role, as they are said to be less likely causal variables. An example of the secondary role of intelligence is given by Gardner (1985a): 'Once students enter into an informal context, their level of intelligence and aptitude will influence how much language material is learned' (p. 148). While this may be the case, it is not impossible that intelligence and aptitude are causally linked with entry into informal language contexts. A high integrative motive and freedom from situational anxiety may not be enough to watch a second language film. Intelligence and aptitude may also influence entry into the experience of the informal context. Such an influence may be less than motivation and situational anxiety; nevertheless intelligence and aptitude could still be causal in a primary sense.

Finally, Gardner (1979, 1983, 1985a) suggests two final outcomes in the four stage model. One outcome concerns bilingual proficiency (fluency, vocabulary and pronunciation, for example); the second outcome refers to non linguistic outcomes such as attitudes, self-concept, cultural values and beliefs. The mention of attitudes suggests that the model is not static but dynamic and cyclical. Outcomes feed back into the model. The experience of the classroom or film affects attitude which affects motivation which, in a never-ending cyclical process, then affects continued experience in the classroom or other environments.

The value of Gardner's (1979, 1983, 1985a) model lies not only in its inclusiveness, but also in that it has been empirically tested using advanced, sophisticated causal modelling techniques (structural equation modelling via LISREL IV). Three studies have investigated whether Gardner's model is empirically valid. Gardner (1983), Gardner et al. (1983) and Lalonde (1982) generally found the model to be valid and powerful in explanation. The LISREL causal modelling technique cannot prove that links are always causal. Nevertheless, given that variables are interactive and that language development is cyclical, the model has been shown to summarise reasonably well important variables and their likely temporal order. The researches also suggested that the integrative attitude was a well defined and important variable in second language proficiency, that personality traits influence attitudes and motivation rather than being a separate and direct contributory cause of achievement. As Gardner (1985a) suggests 'attitude variables are important in that they serve to maintain levels of motivation and that they are not implicated directly in achievement' (p. 158). In one of the researches (Lalonde, 1982) motivation was found to be an indirect cause of achievement. Motivation affected self confidence, with self confidence directly affecting achievement.

The model is not to be seen as final or all-encompassing. As Gardner (1988: 102) argues:

> The model was never intended to be one that would explain all, or even most, of the variance in second language learning because this would ignore the complexity of individuals as well as the language learning task. It was intended simply as a useful heuristic that could explain existing data, suggest possible processes that might be operating in second language learning, and indicate further directions for research.

Research into the Determinants of Language Attitudes

The chapter now moves to consider research which may illuminate the determinants of attitude to a language. Gardner's (1985a) use of language attitude is, in contrast, as a precursor or determinant of language proficiency and use. He admits to its part in a dynamic and not static system. That is, attitude can be an outcome of achievement in a second language, as found by Burstall *et al.* (1974).

The approach to attitude in this book is complementary to Gardner (1985a). It focuses on the factors that may be influential in attitude construction. For example, what factors affect, developmentally, attitude to the Welsh language? What are the causes of a favourable or unfavourable attitude to French in Anglicised areas of Canada?

No model, or even list of factors that may make up attitude to a language has appears to have been drawn up. Therefore this section starts with a list of possible ingredients located separately by previous Welsh research. It then concludes by suggesting how those ingredients may be combined into an overall model that seeks to predict attitude favourability or unfavourability.

Age

One consistent finding from research on attitudes to the Welsh language is that attitude declines with age. Baker's (1988) review of previous research suggested that between 10 and 15 years, attitude to Welsh becomes less favourable. W.R. Jones (1949, 1950), Sharp *et al.* (1973) and E. P. Jones (1982) all found an inverse relationship—as age goes up, favourability of attitude comes down. Sharp *et al.* (1973) also found that as loyalty to Welsh decreases, loyalty to English increases. That is, attitude to English becomes more favourable with increasing age.

This latter research (Sharp *et al.*, 1973) noted that attitude to English may be two dimensional. One dimension relates to the value of English; a second dimension is pivotal on attitude to Welsh. When children held a high degree of loyalty to Welsh, attitude to English became less favourable. That is, attitude to English appeared to be predicated on attitude to Welsh. Sharp *et al.* (1973) conclude: 'when we consider attitude to language in the context of Wales, that attitude towards Welsh is the key variable' (p. 67).

Is English seen in an increasingly utilitarian pragmatic, instrumental manner? Is the universal language of English given increasing status as children get older? Is schooling an important effect—or English and North American television programmes—or youth culture—or employment prospects? Or does the variety of Welsh language cultures have a negative effect on Welsh language attitude? Does age decline in attitude to Welsh reflect a general decline in favourability of a variety of attitudes in the teenage years? Is the movement in minority language attitudes just part of a more general movement in attitudes in the 'adolescent' years, where beliefs and values are re-examined and debated?

The probability is that it is not age that causes language decline. That is, there is not an intrinsic maturational process that creates minority language attitude decline. Rather, it is likely that the socialisation process in adolescence that has an effect. It may be the accompaniments of changing age that are the causes (e.g. heterosexual relationships, mass media influences, influence of peer groups). Age is an 'indicator' or 'holding' variable that sums up movement over time, and does not reveal the underlying reasons for that movement.

Gender

W.R. Jones (1949, 1950), Sharp *et al.* (1973) and E.P. Jones (1982) all found that girls had more favourable attitudes to Welsh than boys. Sharp *et al.* (1973) found this relationship statistically significant at the ages of 10/11, 12/13 and 14/15 with respect to attitude to Welsh, but not for attitude to English.

As with age, this begs the question 'why'? It is again unlikely that the difference is biological or maturational. The reasons for the difference are presumably located in the socio-cultural behaviours of the two gender, and in the kind of individual differences that may exist at any point in history between girls and boys. Are girls more integrative in their attitudes? Do boys find less forms of social status in Welsh culture or Welsh peer groups? Are boys affected by Anglicised 'pop' culture, girls less so?

School

The educational context in which language attitudes develop and change, may be an influencing factor. A school where covert anti-Welsh attitudes are conveyed is likely to have a different effect from schools where the survival and nurturance of Welsh language cultural forms is one prime *raison d'etre*. Both contexts exist in Wales. Catrin Roberts (1985, 1987) found that designated bilingual secondary schools in Wales contain a relatively strong and united sense of commitment and motivation amongst their teachers for Welsh language and Welsh cultural activities (e.g. in extra curricula activity). Such teachers appeared to inculcate integrative attitudes to the Welsh language in their pupils. That is, schools, can in themselves, affect attitudes to a language, be it a majority or minority language. Through the formal or hidden curriculum and through extra curricula activities, a school may produce more or less favourable attitudes and may change attitudes.

Statistical evidence for the effect of designated bilingual schools in Wales comes from Sharp *et al.* (1973). His team found with a large national sample that designated bilingual schools tend to have more favourable attitudes to Welsh than children from a variety of language backgrounds. This is illustrated in Table 2.2.

Table 2.2

	10/11 year olds	11/12 year olds	14/15 year olds
68-81% Welsh speaking neighbourhood	3.97	4.20	4.86
48-55% Welsh speaking neighbourhood	4.22	4.78	5.16
3-26% Welsh speaking neighbourhood	5.39	5.50	5.92
Designated Bilingual Schools	3.21	3.55	3.70

Note: The lower the average score, the more favourable the attitude. (Extracted from Sharp *et al.*, 1973)

The table suggests that children from designated bilingual schools have more favourable attitudes to Welsh than children from Welsh heartland areas. This result is the same across the three age groups. This leads to asking: what is it about such schools that is linked to more favourable attitudes? Are the influential factors not part of school at all? Are the causal factors located with parental values, beliefs and attitudes? Does the peer group, extended family, local community have an influence? Designated bilingual schools in Wales are often the result of parent and community pressure. Designated bilingual schools have tended to attract dedicated and committed teachers (Roberts, 1985). Is this a major influence on favourable attitudes to Welsh? Or is the influence something more abstract, such as the ethos and overall effectiveness of the school? To complicate further, there may be an important interaction between school factors (e.g. teachers, ethos) and out of school factors (e.g. parental attitudes, community pressures). For example, parents may help to provide the resources (e.g. microcomputers) and affect school ethos, even take an active part in school life. Schools and teachers may be influenced by the level of parental interest and support which in turn sways pupil attitudes.

Ability

There is considerable evidence that ability in a language and attitude to that language are linked. From the early research of W.R. Jones (1949, 1950) to the recent modelling of Gardner (1985a), the higher the achievement, proficiency, ability in a language, the more favourable the attitude. One key question in this research is the cause-effect relationship. Does favourable attitude lead to enhanced achievement? Or does greater attainment and proficiency suggest that attitudes cause achievement as indicated by Gardner, Lalonde & Pierson (1983). Burstall et al. (1974) argued for the opposite. In a ten year study of learning French in primary schools in Britain, the partial correlations suggested that early achievement in French more strongly affected later attitudes to French than early attitudes affected later achievement. It is possible that some reciprocal causation also exists. Attitudes and achievement may be both the cause and effect of each other. In a cyclical, spiral relationship, one builds on the other—in an upward or downward relationship. It is also possible that it is the persons perception of proficiency or achievement, and not exam or test scores, that is primarily influential, although the two are obviously related.

Language background

In previous discussions of age, gender and school effects, the possible importance of social-cultural context was highlighted. The language usage of family and friends, community and youth culture, mass media and identification models, peer groups and 'pop' culture may be influential in attitude formation. As Table 2.2 showed, Sharp et al. (1973) found that the Welsh speaking population density in the neighbourhood of a child was related to language attitude. The higher the number of Welsh speakers in a neighbourhood, the more favourable the attitude.

Cultural background

E.P. Jones's (1981) research, further analysed in Baker (1985), found that attitude to Welsh, in particular a decline in attitude to Welsh over the ages

10 to 13, was most linked to various cultural activities. Attendance at Welsh religious services, reading in Welsh and watching English TV appeared the important predictors of attitude decline. A discussion of these results (see Baker, 1985) suggested that being involved in an active participatory Welsh culture was important if attitude to Welsh was to remain favourable. Being actively involved in a Welsh speaking community (e.g. participating in eisteddfodau) was important in maintaining a favourable Welsh attitude.

Six particular variables have been linked by previous research in Wales to attitude formation: age, gender, school, achievement, language background and cultural background. While these may not only be the important variables in effecting language attitudes, they have been located as possibly influential. The issue arises about which variables are more or less important, which interact, which have more or less influential direct and indirect effects? Therefore a model needs to be proposed and tested. The proposal is given in Figure 2.4 and is tested in the next chapter.

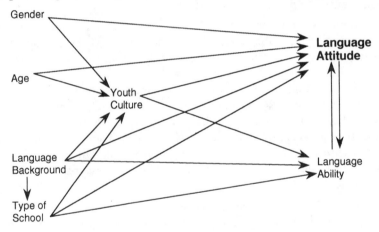

Figure 2.4

The initial model proposed for testing and refinement posits gender, age, language background and school as 'inputs' into an attitude equation. None of these four variables is seen as necessarily influencing the other with one exception. The type of language background from which a pupil derives may affect choice of school. Sometimes, the choice of school does not exist (e.g. in sparsely populated areas). These four variables are then all posited to affect the kind of youth culture experienced. Via youth culture (indirect effect) and directly, these four variables are posited to influence attitude to a language. Youth culture is hypothesised as having a direct effect on attitude. Finally, attitude and ability are regarded as having a mutually reciprocating influence on each other. This model is tested in the next chapter in terms of attitudes to Welsh, and in Chapter 5, in terms of attitude to bilingualism.

This model should not be considered as mechanistic nor static—as is implied in a paper representation of the schema. The model should not be conceived as a snapshot. Rather it needs to be thought of as a film. While gender and school, for example, may be taken as fixed inputs, these are in themselves dynamic, evolving variables. The non- biologicalal aspects of gender (e.g. as expressed in self-concepts of femininity and masculinity) constantly develop and change. While the school as a physical property stays fairly static, the experience and perception of the school changes. Youth culture changes in the teenage years, often with some rapidity. The sum of this is that the models presented need to be seen in individual person terms as dynamic, constantly evolving and being modified. This is partly encapsulated in the final models presented in Chapter 6 which embrace longitudinal measurement. Change in attitude and culture over time are central to these final models.

If continuous evolution within the models is accepted, the models may still suggest a mechanistic action of cause and effect. There is a danger of picturing the models as snooker or pool, with cues hitting the balls which impact on other balls with a final definite outcome. Overt behaviour is not simply caused by a few environmental cues and a few personal variables. To change analogies, it seems more rational to conceive of overt behaviour as a complex collage of numerous interacting effects. A model within this second analogy seeks to deliberately simplify to make sense out of an elaborate, complex, varying and sometimes irregular canvas. It attempts to locate the basic framework of the canvas, the major dynamic elements and their inter-relationship.

What a model disguises is that attitudes are socially constructed particularly through language. Discourse is an important process in the way attitudes are learnt, modified and expressed. The role of language in the construction of attitudes requires a different methodology (e.g. ethnomethodology) to the present approach with a different epistemological basis. Just as there are different ways of painting landscapes, each with something different and important to contribute, so with the art and science of depicting attitudes.

Summary

This chapter has focused on the component parts in building a systems model of language attitudes. The component parts of this model include: a grounding in general attitude theory and research; constructing measurements of attitude and other variables that are reliable and valid; testing for the unidimensionality or multidimensionality of any scales; using multiple variables in a systems model; examining the relationships between variables for interactions, bidirectional links and multiple pathways; and considering contextual features and effects.

Attitude to a specific language is addressed as an example. The tradition of examining such attitudes in terms of instrumental and integrative components has been considered. The Welsh research tradition suggests age, gender, school, ability, language background and cultural background as possible determinants of attitude to the Welsh language. These factors are combined into a three stage model to be tested in research reported in the next chapter.

3 Attitudes and Language: A Research Perspective

Introduction

This chapter attempts to explore by research the concerns of the previous chapter. Through a study of language attitudes, the chapter attempts to move thinking one step further in terms of understanding some of the origins of language attitudes. The chapter also presents one research methodology that may be appropriate for such an advance. The research presented in this chapter evolves from the strong tradition in Wales, Ireland and Scotland that examines the origin of attitudes to the indigenous language (Jones, 1949, 1950; Sharp *et al.*, 1973; E.P Jones, 1982; E.G. Lewis, 1975, 1981; Davies, 1980, 1986 in Wales; CILAR (1975); ÓRiagain & Ó Gliasain, 1984; Fahy, 1988 in Ireland; MacKinnon, 1981 in Scotland).

Previous research tends to be bivariate. That is, it looks at attitude to a language and one other variable at a time. For example, Celtic language attitude research has focused on the following as separate issues:

- language attitude and gender
- language attitude and age
- language attitude and ability or achievement
- language attitude and language background
- language attitude and type of school attended
- language attitude and social class

It was argued in the previous chapter that a more sophisticated and sensitive approach is to move from simple descriptions of relationships, to considering all the variables at one go. One overall analysis of a model of language attitudes should reveal which variables affect language attitudes in major and minor ways. Is gender less influential than the language (or languages) spoken at home and in the community? Does school or age have a larger effect on change on language attitudes during adolescence?

The Choice of Variables

A piece of research was undertaken to explore language attitudes. The research, sponsored by the Economic and Social Research Council (ESRC), commenced with 797 children from three different types of school in North and Mid Wales. The first decision was to build on the foundations of previous Celtic language attitude research by selecting five variables known to relate to the origin of language attitudes, i.e.

• Gender
• Age
• Language Background
• Type of School
• Ability in Welsh

The second decision was to use the input-context-output model considered in Baker (1985, 1988). From the above list, gender and age tend to be relatively 'fixed' inputs. There is no choice or freedom about such individual characteristics. Similarly, language background and type of school attended comprise 'fixed' contexts. There is little or no choice by children in terms of living in such environments.

One source of influence on language attitudes has been missing from most previous research. There are chosen contexts where people's language attitudes may be tested, enacted and influenced. The kind of institutional cultural affiliation that, for example, teenagers choose may affect the favourability or unfavourability of their language attitudes. Teenagers may choose from a variety of cultural contexts—each of which may affect attitudes, especially attitudes to a minority language and culture. Discos and dating, books and baseball, popular music and parties, church and concerts are just a few varied contexts where teenagers' language attitudes may be reinforced, changed, challenged and developed.

The concept and definition of youth culture is complex and open to debate. The preferred notion of youth culture is from social psychology.

> By the culture of a group of people is meant their whole way of life—their language, ways of perceiving, categorising and thinking about the world, forms of non-verbal communication and social interaction, rules and conventions about behaviour, moral values and ideals, technology and material culture, art science, literature and history. All these aspects of culture affect social behaviour, directly or indirectly. (Argyle, 1983)

The operalisation of youth culture in this research is necessarily a restricted version of this definition. The contexts in which culture is enacted are taken as an indicator of youth culture. Such cultural contexts (e.g.

youth clubs, sports, peer relationships) are referred to as youth culture. However, the measurement of youth culture (see Appendix 1) is a partial and restricted notion of the entity.

The use of the input–context–output model in planning research raises the issue of sequence of variables. The issue is simply, what affects what? Does language attitude determine choice of youth culture? Does youth culture determine language attitudes? Are language attitudes both affected by, and affect cultural contexts? That is, is there a mutual cause—effect, circular relationship? Is the chicken–egg question not resolvable?

A model can first be posed. This model will suggest a possible sequence of causation, usually by attention to chronological sequencing. Then, secondly, the model can be tested statistically (e.g. by structural equation modelling), to see if the sequencing is suitable or not. Testing the model may reveal a wrong presupposition, a relationship in the wrong direction, a mutually reciprocating relationship where none had been posited. An example of a potential cause–effect specification problem is between ability and language attitudes. What causes what? What is the correct temporal sequence? Or is one both the cause and effect of the other? Do both need to be regarded as outputs in the model?

The initial model posited is shown as Figure 3.1. The arrows show the direction of causation to be tested.

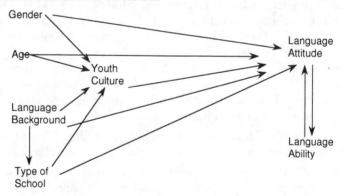

Figure 3.1

The model suggests that:

(i) Gender, age, language background and type of school directly affect attitude to a language, as does youth culture.

(ii) Gender, age, language background and type of school also indirectly affect language attitudes through youth culture. That is, these variables affect choice of youth culture, which in turn affects attitudes to a language.

(iii) Ability and attitude to a language form a two way 'cause–effect' process and both are outputs in the model.

Testing this model should reveal if the variables are inclusive enough to explain differences in the origins of attitude to a language. That is, are there other variables, not included in this model, that are needed to account adequately for differences in language attitudes?

The Measurement of the Variables

Measurement of the variables in the model was achieved by the construction of a series of short 'scales' for the chosen sample. A bilingual test booklet was compiled (see Appendix 1) and contained the following measures:

A youth culture contexts scale

This scale had been developed previously by Baker & Waddon (1987, 1990). It comprises 25 items and seeks to elicit patterns in the way teenagers spend their free time e.g. :

Item 1 – Go to a Youth club.

Item 2 – Go to a Church/Chapel.

Responses are made on a 5 point scale from Very Often to Never

Language background

This 21 item scale was newly constructed from a variety of previous scales (Jones, 1966; Sharp et al., 1973; Linguistics Minorities Project, 1985). Such scales and their criticisms were discussed by Baker & Hinde (1984)— and it was partly out of the discussion in that article that the present scale was compiled (see Appendix 1).

Age and gender

A short questionnaire at the end of the test booklet elicited details of age and gender; 43.5% of the sample were girls, 56.5% boys. The age structure of the initial sample is shown in Figure 3.2.

Schools

Three schools were chosen to represent three distinct types of school in Wales. First, a school in a Welsh heartland area was selected. This 'natural' Welsh secondary (age 11 to 18) school is situated in an area where, accord-

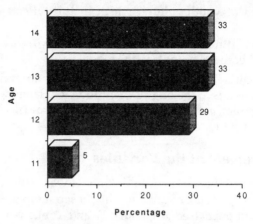

Figure 3.2 Distribution of age

ing to the 1981 Census, over 70% of the population speak Welsh (see Baker, 1985). While being a 'natural' Welsh school, it experienced an influx of in-migrants before and during the research. Such children tend to be monolingual English and thus constitute a small and different sub-group within that school.

Second, a designated 'Ysgolion Cymraeg' was selected. Such secondary (age 11 to 18) schools are sited in predominantly Anglicised areas of Wales. This school was placed in an area where Anglicised culture is dominant. The pupils of the school come from varied language backgrounds. Most pupils derive from Welsh speaking homes from a wide catchment area. A small number of pupils come from homes where English speaking parents have chosen to have their children educated through the medium of Welsh (immersion bilingual education).

Third, an English medium secondary (age 11 to 18) school was selected, being situated in an area where less than 1 in 10 people speak Welsh. While the medium of instruction in the two previous schools is mostly Welsh, in the third school, the curriculum is delivered in English. Welsh was (at the time of the research) taught as a second language for three years and thereafter became an option.

The schools were chosen as representing three different types of 'Welsh' school. One has a strong and long tradition of 'Welshness'. It is placed in a community that is supportive of traditional Welsh cultural forms. Another has relatively recently been established and has evolved from small beginnings into a seemingly flourishing institution. It serves a catchment area that is predominantly English speaking and Anglo in culture. However, its clientele are possibly no less fervently Welsh than the 'natural' Welsh school. The third school serves a clientele who mostly appear to regard themselves as being from Wales but without the heritage language and culture. The actual language background composition of the schools is presented in Table 3.1. (The four language background categories are discussed in detail later in this chapter).

Table 3.1 Language background

School	Dominant Welsh	Bilingual Welsh Bias	Bilingual English Bias	Dominant English
Designated Bilingual	15.5%	30.6%	52.8%	1.1%
'Natural' Welsh	39.8%	20.3%	18.8%	21.1%
English-medium	0.7%	0.0%	1.1%	98.1%

The 'Natural Welsh' school contains a variety of language backgrounds. One in five children are from 'English-only' language contexts (many of these are in-migrants). Although traditionally a 'Welsh' school, the intake appears to create initially a less Welsh school than the designated bilingual school. The designated bilingual school draws its clients from bilingual rather than Welsh environments, with only 1 in a 100 coming from an English-only context.

A caution must be sounded. While the three schools have been labelled as 'natural' Welsh, designated bilingual and English-medium, such labels hide a variety of other characteristics about the schools. Such characteristics may not be about 'Welshness' or language and may additionally, or alternatively, explain differences found between these schools which are presented later. For example, differences in social class composition of the schools, the degree of enthusiasm and commitment of teachers in preserving the Welsh language and culture (see Roberts, 1985,1987) or the ex-curricula activity of the school may also, or alternatively, explain differences between these schools.

'Types of school' is a bland, generalised label. The dimensions along which schools differ are many (e.g. Mortimore *et al.*, 1988; Smith & Tomlinson, 1989). The differences of label used in this research indicate just one major area of difference. An aim of further research must be to relate various dimensions of classroom and school differences to outcome variables (e.g. by hierarchical modelling, Baker, 1990b; Goldstein, 1987).

Ability

A difficulty in measuring ability or achievement was encountered in this and previous research (Baker & Waddon, 1990). Across the three schools, no comparable, standard data existed. School examination marks for 11 to

14 year olds are only understandable within a school, even within a stream or set. Since different age-groups were used in the study, no examination results were available which enabled comparisons of all respondents to be made. Ability in Welsh was the target variable. No usable standardised test was available to measure Welsh language ability. Teacher ratings and pupil ratings become an imperfect alternative. Asking teachers to rate the children would have presented problems. Differences in the curriculum across teachers and across schools would have made teacher-ratings in these circumstances, inappropriate and invalid. Therefore pupil self-ratings was chosen—based on use in previous research (Baker & Waddon, 1990). Previous research revealed a near normal distribution of responses and a variable with construct and predictive validity. Baker & Waddon (1990) discuss the problems of comparability and compatibility in pupil self- ratings and the problems of self-deceit, social desirability and self-knowledge. The question appeared at the end of the test booklet (see Appendix 1).

A decision was made to ask respondents to rate themselves in terms of five categories. While some pupils may tend to exaggerate, (and some pupils may underestimate) their ability in Welsh, the resulting quasi-normal distribution gives an indication that some credence may be attached to the pupils' replies to this question.

Near the bottom in Welsh	17.3%
Below average in Welsh	23.3 %
About average in Welsh	50.4 %
Better than average in Welsh	6.6 %
Near the top in Welsh	2.4 %

This question yields only an approximate indication of individual pupils' ability. Apart from the problem of under and over estimation, there is the problem of 'average compared with whom?'. The notion of 'average' may not be the same in the three schools, nor in different sets and streams within the same school. Also, the question only refers to Welsh. Other curriculum areas were not analysed.

Attitude to language

Two different 'attitude to the Welsh language' scales were composed. The first is the traditional attitude to language questionnaire (e.g. Jones, 1966; Sharp et al., 1973 (a Thurstone Scale); E.P. Jones, 1982). Examples of items are :

Item 4: It's a waste of time to keep the Welsh language alive

Item 12: Welsh is essential to take part fully in Welsh life

Answers ranged from 'strongly agree' to 'strongly disagree' on a 5 point scale. This traditional attitude scale comprised 20 items (see Appendix 1).

The second attitude inventory concerned 'use, value and status' attitudes to the Welsh language. Examples of the 20 items are :

How important or unimportant do you think the Welsh language is for people to do the following?

Item 2: To earn plenty of money

Item 17: Be accepted in the community

A minor issue in the research was to investigate how the two different scales performed. The initial expectation, following the discussions in chapter one, was that the second 'use, value and status' questionnaire might prove more reliable and fruitful in its relationship with other variables in the model. This is due to the more definable level of generality of the 'use, value and status' approach, and due to the more concrete, less abstract approach of the statements. The original intention of the research was also to measure attitude to English (as in Sharp *et al.*, 1973). Pragmatic and political difficulties militated against the inclusion of attitude to English scales.

The Passage of the Research

Pupils from the three schools were tested twice with an interval of two years. The results of the second testing become the subject of Chapter 6 where change in attitudes are examined. For the purposes of this chapter and the next, the initial results form the main focus. Of the 797 pupils tested at the beginning of the research, 256 came from the 'natural' Welsh school, 270 from the designated bilingual school and the remainder, 271, from the English medium school. These pupils were initially tested when in the first, second and third year of secondary education, and then again when in the third, fourth and fifth year.

Between testings, 140 pupils were 'lost' (the ill-phrased experimental mortality rate being 17.7%). Most pupils 'lost' had either moved from the school or were away from school at the second testing. Such 'loss' only affects the results of the final chapter.

Scaling

Gender, age, type of school and ability in Welsh were immediately usable as variables. Language background, Youth Culture and the two language attitude scales each contained 20 or more items. To ensure the scales are internally consistent and will discriminate between differing strengths of attitude, some form of item analysis is normally performed. The Likert, Thurstone & Guttman techniques for attitude scales, for example, attempt to remove items which are poor discriminators between different viewpoints. Alternatively, measures of internal consistency (e.g. Cronbach's alpha) and item-total correlations are used to sort out the good from the less good items.

In addition to constructing a scale from the better items, it is important to investigate whether the items within a scale are measuring one or two or more entities. That is, is the scale unidimensional or multidimensional? Language attitude theory suggests two dimensions—integrative and instrumental (see Chapter 2). Previous analyses of the Youth Culture questionnaire also suggested multidimensionality (Baker & Waddon, 1990).

The preference is to submit the items of each scale to a latent variable analysis. The outcome of latent variable analysis is an indication of whether there are one or more dimensions to the scale. The process also provides a latent variable score for each pupil on the dimension(s). This score is based on a weighting of items to increase consistency, discrimination and validity. The preferable term for the resulting scale is a latent variable rather than a factor scale (Bartholomew,1987). This term accurately conveys the idea that something underlying is being measured. The phenomena being considered are hypothetical. The term latent variable contains the idea that a representation has been assembled, from a variety of indicators, of a hypothetical, underlying variable. A more technical expression of the procedure followed occurs in Appendix 2.

The use of latent variable analysis resulted in the following scales. First, the Youth Culture items (see Appendix 1) were submitted to latent variable analysis. This suggested the presence of two dimensions. These two dimensions are listed below with item weightings above 0.30.

Youth Culture : Welsh Traditional & Literary Culture

Read books out of school	0.59
Go to Eisteddfodau (Welsh cultural events)	0.59
Go to Yr Urdd (Welsh League of Youth)	0.54
Go to a Library	0.54
Shopping	0.39
Go to Church/Chapel	0.38
Walking	0.32
Visit Relatives	0.32

Youth Culture - Popular Culture

Opposite Sex Friendships	0.62
Go to discos	0.58
Play Records / Cassettes	0.53
Same Sex Friendships	0.46
Shopping	0.40
Read Newspapers	0.33
Watch TV / Videos	0.31
Read Magazines / comics	0.31

Language Background (one latent variable)

A Language Background variable was created by latent variable analysis of the 21 items in the Language Background questionnaire (see Appendix 1). The analysis suggested that the 21 items best fitted one dimension. On the unrotated latent variable matrix, the 21 items loaded between 0.62 and 0.92 on the latent variable. That is, all items had high weightings on the latent variable and contributed as follows:

In which language do YOU speak to the following people?

1. Father	0.90
2. Mother	0.91
3. Brothers / Sisters	0.93
4. Friends in the Classroom	0.84
5. Friends outside School	0.83
6. Teachers	0.66
7. Friends in the Playground	0.85
8. Neighbours (near my house)	0.79

In which language do the following people speak to you?

1. Father	0.89
2. Mother	0.90
3. Brother / Sisters	0.92
4. Friends in the Classroom	0.82
5. Friends outside School	0.80
6. Teachers	0.62
7. Friends in the Playground	0.83
8. Neighbours (near my house)	0.79

Which language do YOU use with the following?

1. Watching T.V. / Videos	0.80
2. Church / Chapel	0.86
3. Newspapers / Comics / Magazines	0.74
4. Records / Cassettes	0.67
5. Radio	0.81

Following the procedure outlined in Baker & Hinde (1984), a cluster analysis was also performed on the language background data. Such a method places people rather than test items into groups. Just as stars are not randomly distributed in the heaven but form clusters, so groups of similar people emerge. This analysis suggested the presence of four groups in terms of language background (see Figure 3.3).

1. Dominantly Welsh language pupils (*N* = 146)
2. Dominantly English language pupils (*N* = 322)
3. Bilinguals with a bias towards Welsh (*N* = 135)
4. Bilinguals with a bias towards English (*N* = 194)

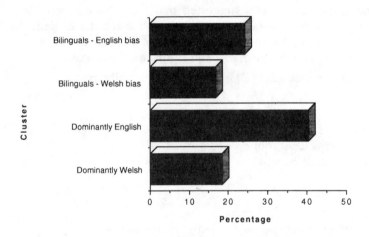

Figure 3.3 Language background

Attitude to the Welsh Language (General Scale)

One latent variable only was found, with 16 out of the 20 items loading over 0.30. The items excluded by virtue of their low loadings were items 6, 11, 16 and 17. The highest loadings were found on the following items :

I prefer to be taught in Welsh	0.84
Welsh is a language worth learning	0.80
I like speaking Welsh	0.80
If I have children, I would like them to be Welsh speaking	0.80

Attitude to the Welsh Language (Use, Value and Status)

Two dimensions were located by latent variable analysis. As the following list of items of the two latent variables reveals, these two latent variables fit the instrumental and integrative distinction.

(i) Integrative Attitude to Welsh

Item 18	Talk to friends in school	0.76
Item 20	Talk to people out of school	0.71
Item 1	To make friends	0.69
Item 12	Play sport	0.62
Item 4	Write	0.59
Item 3	Read	0.58
Item 8	Be liked	0.56
Item 19	Talk to teachers at school	0.50

(ii) Instrumental Attitude

Item 7	Become cleverer	0.64
Item 6	Get a job	0.63
Item 2	To earn plenty of money	0.60
Item 16	Pass exams	0.55
Item 14	Go shopping	0.43
Item 8	Be liked	0.42

Reliabilities

As expressed in the previous chapter, the reliability of measurement is important. Following the latent variable analysis, the alpha reliability coefficient of the latent variable scales was computed. The results were:

Youth Culture - Popular Culture	0.65
Youth Culture - Welsh Culture	0.67
Language Background	0.98
Attitude to the Welsh Language - General	0.93
Attitude to the Welsh Language - Use, Value and Status	
(a) Instrumental	0.92
(b) Integrative	0.88
(Attitude to Bilingualism - see next chapter)	0.89

The attitude scales and the language background scale are of acceptable reliability (above 0.85). The Youth culture scales are below the 0.85 level— possibly needing more items to ensure internal consistency. These relia- bilities were introduced into the various models of language attitudes, details of which follow later in this chapter.

Initial Explorations

Before examining the model that has been posed, it is valuable and important to look at the simple descriptive statistics. There is often a danger of missing important information by immediately moving to multivariate techniques (e.g. LISREL, ANOVA, Discriminant Analysis). Simple frequencies, percentages, means and graphs appropriately analysed, often contain a wealth of information.

General attitudes

Of the twenty items in the general attitude to Welsh scale, 12 items tended to elicit definite 'agree' or 'disagree' viewpoints. The sample as a whole tended to AGREE with the following items (i.e. agree was the modal response).

- Welsh should be taught to all pupils in Wales
- I like speaking Welsh
- I'm likely to use Welsh as an adult
- Welsh is a language worth learning
- Welsh has a place in the modern world
- We need to preserve the Welsh language
- It's hard to study Science in Welsh
- If I have children, I would like them to be Welsh speaking

Except for the 'study Science in Welsh' item, the overall attitudes of the sample were favourable to the Welsh language. The sample disagreed that 'Welsh is a difficult language to learn', 'You are considered a lower class person if you speak Welsh' and that they 'prefer to watch TV in Welsh'. There was strong disagreement with the statement 'It's a waste of time to keep the Welsh language alive'. Such negative responses to negative statements about the Welsh language (except for the TV item) confirm that these 11 to 14 year olds are generally supportive of the Welsh language.

The profile of the second attitude to Welsh scale (the use, value, importance or status of the Welsh language) provides the following rank order of importance given to that language:

Order of (Mean) Importance	Item	Modal Response
1st	Pass Exams	Important
2nd	Get a Job	Important
3rd	Talk to Teachers in School	Important
4th	Write	Important
5th	Be Accepted in the Community	Important
6th	Become Cleverer	Important
7th	Live in Wales	Important
8th	Read	Important
9th	Bring up Children	Important
10th	To make Friends	A little Important
11th	Talk to Friends in School	Important

12th	Go to Church/Chapel	Important
13th	To earn plenty of money	A little Important
14th	Go shopping	A little Important
15th	Talk to people out of school	Important
16th	Sing (e.g. with others)	A little Important
17th	Make phone calls	A little Important
18th	Go shopping	A little Important
19th	Play Sport	Unimportant
20th	Watch TV/Videos	Unimportant

Higher mean values were given to a mixture of instrumental (e.g. pass exams, get a job) and integrative attitudes (e.g. be accepted in the community), with a bias towards instrumental attitudes as being more valued. Eighteen out of twenty items obtained 'important' or 'a little important' as the most frequently occurring category. This suggests there exists a good deal of support for the Welsh language in this age group. Two items, 'play sport' and 'watch TV/videos' were both regarded as 'unimportant' for the Welsh language. These are two major domains of youth culture where the Welsh language appears to be given little or no value by the respondents.

Gender and ability differences

No gender or ability differences were found on the three attitude to Welsh language scales (hereafter termed General attitude, Integrative attitude and Instrumental attitude). Parenthetically, it can be stated that this is not due to the three attitude scales measuring the same entity. Integrative and instrumental attitudes to the use, value, status and importance of Welsh were separated by latent variable analysis and the general attitude dimension only correlated 0.37 and 0.21 respectively with these two scales. No gender or ability differences across the three scales attests to some consistency in this finding with this sample of pupils.

Age differences

On each of the three scales of language attitude, a statistically significant relationship ($p < 0.001$) was found with age. Consistent across the integrative and instrumental attitude scales was the considerable change that occurred between 13 and 14 years of age. Integrative and instrumental attitudes became less favourable in the third form of secondary schooling. Figures 3.4 and 3.5 illustrate this.

As the graphs show, while there is a downward movement from 11 years to 14 years of age, the significant difference is between 13 and 14 years of age. This movement may coincide with the advance of adolescence (although not all teenagers go through 'adolescence'). Motivational and

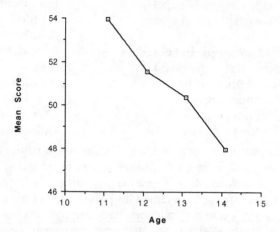

Figure 3.4 Integrative attitude

Note: Language Attitude Means are derived from latent variable scores converted to 'T' scores, with a Mean of 50 and Standard deviation of 10. The Students–Newman–Keuls (SNK) procedure indicated that the significant difference was between 14 year olds and 11/12/13 year olds combined.

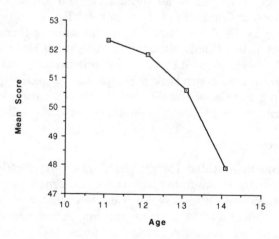

Figure 3.5 Instrumental attitude to Welsh

Note: SNK Test revealed that the significant difference was between 14 year olds and 11/12/13 year olds.

physical changes, the growth of Piagetian formal operations, changes in self concept, the move away from family identity towards more individual and peer group identity may be connected to attitude to Welsh becoming less favourable. This is explored further in the model. It is also possible that age changes in language attitude are part of a general decline in favourability of attitude (e.g. to school) that may occur in the teenage years. In this sense, attitude to language changes may not be special or isolated, but need to be related to the changes of the teenage years.

With general attitude to Welsh, a less strong relationship was found with age. The correlations, set out below, confirm this.

Correlation of   Age and Integrative Attitude = -0.18

                        Age and Instrumental Attitude = -0.18

Correlation of   Age and General Attitude = -0.08

One reason for the lower correlation may be found in the theoretical discussion of attitudes in the first chapter. Attitude measurement may work better when items concern specific events rather than wide generalities. The use, value, status, importance of Welsh attitude scales concerns concrete events (reading, exams, talking to friends). This instrumental and integrative scales concern attitude to the use of Welsh in concrete situations. The general attitude to Welsh scale is the traditional form. The items are sometimes more abstract, more about ideas, more general (e.g. 'We need to preserve the Welsh language', 'Welsh should be taught to all pupils in Wales').

With general attitude to Welsh, the only statistically significant difference was between 13 and 14 year olds. No other pairs of year groups had significantly different means. This again suggests that the period between 13 and 14 years of age is a critical one in terms of language attitude decline. This finding replicates the finding from W.R. Jones (1949, 1950) in the 1940s, Sharp et al. (1973) in the late 1960s and E.P. Jones (1982) in the late 1970s and early 1980s. However over these decades, the critical period of decline appears to have changed. W.R. Jones's (1950) research suggested that the critical period of decline was between 14 and 15 years of age. This chapter has suggested 13 to 14 as the critical change period.

Contexts: Type of school and language background

The initial analysis looked simply for differences between the three schools and then, separately, between children from different types of language background.

First, across the three language attitude scales, the consistent finding was that the English medium school pupils had less favourable attitudes to Welsh than those from the natural Welsh and designated bilingual schools. Between these latter two schools, there was no statistically significant difference.

Second, language background was related to all three language attitude scales. On the general attitude scale and the integrative scale, all four language background groups were different from each other. In the ordering below, the higher the mean, the more favourable the attitude.

(a) General attitude

Language Background	Mean Score
1. Predominantly Welsh	60.4
2. Bilingual - Biased to Welsh	54.8
3. Bilingual - Biased to English	50.9
4. Predominantly English	42.6
	$(r = 0.70)$

(b) Integrative attitude

Language Background	Mean Score
1. Predominantly Welsh	56.5
2. Bilingual - Welsh bias	52.7
3. Bilingual - English bias	50.3
4. Predominantly English	45.7
	$(r = 0.46)$

Thus, the more Welsh the language background, the more favourable the attitude to Welsh. The two correlations of 0.70 and 0.46 attest to this strong relationship. The instrumental attitude scale showed a marginally significant relationship with the language background latent variable ($r = -0.08$; $p = 0.08$). This was unexpected. The 'fit' with the previous results would suggest a strong positive relationship between a favourable instrumental attitude to Welsh and coming from a Welsh language background. The results suggested (by the SNK test), that a difference could be located between the groups shown in Figure 3.6.

A relatively more favourable instrumental attitude to Welsh was found in the predominantly Welsh than the predominantly English group—as expected. However, a relatively high mean is held by the pupils from predominantly English bilingual backgrounds. Such pupils seem to be aware more than their 'nearest' group (English only), that Welsh can be the passport to career and monetary rewards and has a functional usage outside of social encounters. For a minority language, this seems a silver lining to the grey cloud. In a group that might be moving towards the

Figure 3.6

majority language, there is apparent awareness of a minority language as instrumentally valuable.

A further important consideration is the possibility of interactions between background variables. Chapter 2 discussed this and provided an example. A variety of analyses were run to try to detect iterations (by 2 way and 3 way ANOVAs). No significant interactions were found between pairs or triplets of any background (input and context) variables.

Youth cultural contexts

Youth cultural contexts are represented in the form of two latent variables. Each of these was correlated with the three attitude scales. Table 3.2 presents these correlations.

Table 3.2

	Youth Culture I Welsh Traditional and Literary Cultural contexts	*Youth Culture II* Popular Culture
General Attitude to Welsh	0.44	-0.17
Integrative Attitude to Welsh	0.34	-0.13
Instrumental Attitude to Welsh	0.02	0.01

The correlations suggest that youth cultural contexts and instrumental attitude are not related. A pattern of teenage behaviour which is concerned with traditional Welsh culture (e.g. attending eisteddfodau and chapel) and literacy tends to be connected with holding a favourable integrative attitude to the Welsh language. Being involved in 'popular' culture tends to be related to a less favourable attitude to the integrative value of Welsh, as expressed in the negative correlation. A similar, and slightly stronger pattern, is found with general attitude to Welsh. A positive attitude to Welsh tends to be found where someone engages in traditional forms of Welsh culture and is bookish. A less positive attitude is found amongst those who tend towards the 'popular' culture of records, discos and gregariousness in peer groups.

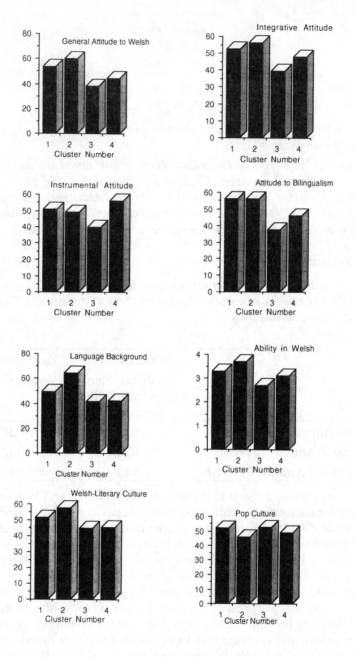

Figure 3.7

Patterns of attitude

One way of understanding pupils' attitudes is to attempt to locate groups of similar pupils. Similar people may form distinctive groups. Are there groups of children in this sample who share similar characteristics? Are these groups distinctive from each other in an identifiable way? Based on the information collected at the first testing, a cluster analysis was performed. The analysis suggested that the 797 pupils fitted into four well defined groups. When profiled across eight variables, four distinct patterns of pupils were found. This profile is illustrated in the eight histograms in Figure 3.7.

Group One pupils numbered 264. The designated bilingual school children were predominantly located in this group. The group displayed average scores on the youth culture latent variables, on the Welshness of language background and instrumental attitudes to Welsh. What is particularly notable in this first group is an above average favourable attitude to Welsh and bilingualism (details regarding attitude to bilingualism are given in the following chapter). Here is a group, some without a particularly Welsh background, but who have developed particularly favourable attitudes to the Welsh language and to bilingualism.

Group Two pupils numbered 171, and originate from relatively strong 'Welsh' language backgrounds. Many appear to derive from 'heartland' Welsh areas and are mostly located in the natural Welsh school. The group are very favourable in their attitude to Welsh, attitude to bilingualism and in their integrative attitudes. They are less likely to engage in popular culture and more likely to participate in Welsh cultural and literary activities. Instrumental attitude to Welsh is average for the group, and ability in Welsh relatively high. In none of the four groups did there appear any particular gender bias. Group two pupils tend to fit the image of traditional, rural, Welsh children. The customary image of such children has one surprise. The instrumental attitude to Welsh is average (49.1 compared with a standardised 'T' score mean of 50.0). These 'heartland' children tend to value Welsh for its integrative and affiliative value. Are there doubts about the value of Welsh for academic vocational success? Is Welsh seen as the language of the home and hearth and not of mobility and money? Is Welsh perceived as valuable for chapel and culture, and not for factory and finance?

Group Three contains 124 pupils, the smallest of the groups. This is the only group with an age difference. More of this group are older than average. Interested in popular culture, not interested in books, their attitudes to Welsh and bilingualism are relatively less favourable. Integrative and instrumental attitudes are both comparatively low, as is ability in

Welsh. There appears to be little Welsh about this group other than their geographic location in Wales.

Group Four of 238 pupils is like group three, but with one notable difference. Similar to group three, their language background is distinctly English, with attitude to Welsh and bilingualism being relatively less favourable. Integrative attitudes to Welsh are also below average. The difference between this group and group three is their high instrumental attitude to Welsh. Of the four groups, their 'instrumental' mean is the only one well above average. Coming mostly, but not exclusively from the English medium school, Welsh is seen exclusively for its instrumental, utilitarian value. Here is a group from almost exclusively English medium backgrounds who see the Welsh language as valuable in functional terms. This is in distinct comparison with the most Welsh group whose instrumental attitude to Welsh is comparatively less strong.

Summary

So far in the results, attitude appears more strongly connected with the 'environmental' variables than individual attributes. Language background and youth culture appear more strongly correlated to language attitude than gender, age and ability. Environmental pulls and pushes may affect attitudes in terms of the language heard and spoken in various domains. Particularly critical may be the youth peer group. The values, culture and activities of that group may affect attitude to Welsh, especially at 13 to 14 years of age. The nature and strengths of these associations, however, is better tested in the model.

The Model

The variables considered so far can now be combined into one overall analysis. The testing of the model enables the detection of major and minor effects in the determination of attitudes. A model is constructed by consideration of the direction of likely causality and of direct and indirect effects. Some examples will explain and illustrate.

Attitude to the Welsh language clearly does not affect someone's age. Rather the reverse is possible. In diagrammatic form this becomes:

Age → Attitude to Welsh

In this diagram, the posited cause–effect is indicated by the direction of the arrow. However, this pattern may be too simple. Older children may develop a less favourable attitude as they grow older due to their experience of youth culture. Age, in this case, in an indirect effect. Its influence is mediated by an intervening variable. A diagram to represent this becomes:

Age → Youth Culture → Attitude to Welsh

A third diagram is possible, representing age as being a direct and an indirect effect on attitude to Welsh:

Finally, it is conceivable that reciprocal causation can occur. For example, youth culture may affect attitude to Welsh. Attitude to Welsh may also affect the choice of youth culture. This pattern, where one variable is both the cause and the effect of the other, may be represented thus:

The overall model to be tested is now re-presented in Figure 3.8.

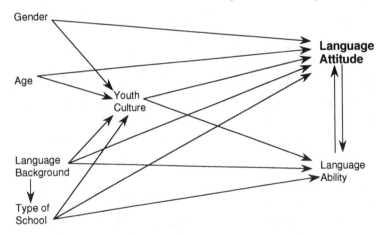

Figure 3.8

This model suggests that language attitudes are directly and indirectly affected by gender, age, language background, type of school, Welsh/Literary cultural contexts and popular culture. Language ability is posited to have a direct effect on language attitudes, with such attitudes reciprocally affecting language ability. The model above was tested for each of the three attitude scales in turn, and in one overall model. During the testing process, the models were systematically explored and refined. Details of this occur in Appendix 2. The results of the testing and refining process are now presented in simplified form to highlight the substantial rather than the statistical issues. The full version of the final models is given in Appendix 2, complete with disturbance terms. Three simplified final models are now presented in Figures 3.9 and 3.10—one for each attitude scale.

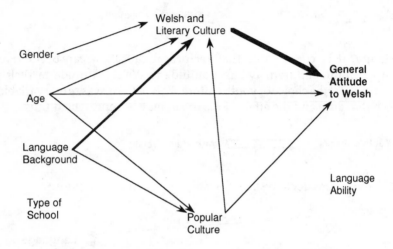

Note: The model shows the paths with coefficients over 0.25. The thickness of the arrows represents the strength of association. Full details in Appendix 2.

Figure 3.9 Summary of Effects on General Attitude to Welsh

	Total	Indirect
Gender	0.004	0.23
Age	–0.01	–0.37
Language Background	0.75	0.83
Type of School	0.15	–0.07
Welsh and Literary Culture	0.93	0.02
Popular Culture	–0.06	0.26
Ability in Welsh	0.16	n/a

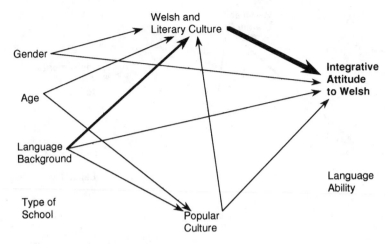

Note: The model shows the paths with coefficients over 0.25. The thickness of the arrows represents the strength of association.

Figure 3.10 Summary of Effects on Integrative Attitude to Welsh

	Total	Indirect
Gender	–0.05	0.23
Age	–0.15	–0.36
Language Background	0.49	0.74
Type of School	–0.01	–0.07
Welsh and Literary Culture	0.91	0.00
Popular Culture	–0.04	0.26
Ability in Welsh	–0.03	n/a

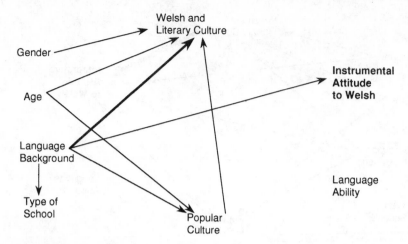

Paths represented are all over 0.20.

Figure 3.11 Summary of Effects on Instrumental Attitude to Welsh

	Total	Indirect
Gender	0.03	0.05
Age	–0.22	–0.05
Language Background	–0.11	0.12
Type of School	–0.05	–0.01
Welsh and Literary Culture	0.14	0.01
Popular Culture	0.04	0.05
Ability in Welsh	0.11	n/a

The fit of the models

The presentation of the results suggests seven outcomes in terms of the original hypothesised specification of the model.

(1) Generally, the model as posited was correct. However, a few alterations are necessary.

(2) A relationship between Popular culture and Welsh and literary cultural affiliation was a particularly important addition to the posited model to achieve an acceptable fit.

(3) Ability in Welsh appeared to influence attitude to Welsh. The opposite way round (attitude affecting ability) and a mutually reciprocal causation was not required or demanded by the model.

(4) The general attitude model and the integrative attitude model provided reasonably acceptable statistical solutions. Both accounted for an appreciable amount of variance.

(5) The instrumental model was not satisfactory—with the proportion of unexplained variance being 0.93. To explain instrumental attitudes, other 'absent' variables will be needed (and a more reliable measurement of instrumental attitude). Therefore, no further consideration of instrumental attitude is given in this chapter.

(6) The disturbance terms are revealing—and are presented in the full model in Appendix 2. The disturbance term refers to the effect of unknown variables, the effect of known but omitted variables, the randomness of human behaviour and measurement error. The disturbance terms located that ability in Welsh, Popular culture and Instrumental attitudes may need improved measurement or definition. The measurement of language background, Welsh and Literary culture and general attitude is relatively satisfactory. Type of school has a disturbance term of 0.94, hinting that the 'umbrella' terms hides a number of more crucial, causal variables, as discussed earlier in this chapter.

(7) An overall model, using the three attitudes combined into one latent 'language attitude' variable (see Appendix 2) was tested. While such an overall model rests on the assumption that the three attitude scales should be reduced to one latent variable, the results are similar to the general attitude and integrative attitude analyses.

Implications

The implications of the models may be summarised as follows:

(1) The single strongest influence on language attitudes is Welsh and Literary culture. Being immersed in eisteddfodau, organised Welsh language youth activities (e.g. Yr Urdd—the Welsh League of Youth), and reading books out of school appeared as the most influential determinants of a favourable attitude to Welsh.

(2) The second strongest influence on language attitudes was language background. It was expected that the language of the home, peer group and community would be a strong influence on attitude. It was not necessarily predictable that Welsh and Literary culture would be more strongly related to attitude than language background. Language background also affected attitudes indirectly. Through influencing immersion in Welsh and Literary culture and through influencing popular culture activity, language background affected attitudes indirectly, as well as directly.

(3) Gender and Age were also influences on attitude, with girls and younger pupils having a more favourable attitude. Such influences tend to be indirect (through effects on cultural activity) rather than direct on language attitudes. Age appears to be a stronger influence than gender.

(4) Immersion in popular culture had a definite negative influence on attitude to Welsh. Such popular culture also affects language attitudes indirectly through its negative effect on involvement in Welsh language and literary culture. This theme is returned to in more detail in the sixth chapter.

(5) Ability in Welsh and the type of school attended appear to have a relatively negligible effect on language attitudes. However, alternative explanations are possible. The disturbance terms reveal the need for more precise specification of each variable and improved measurement. In terms of type of school, the small number of schools used and the focus on language difference between the schools is a limitation. A larger number of schools, differentiated on a wider selection of variables is needed to examine more accurately the effect of schools on language attitude. Multilevel modelling is required, integrated with structural equation modelling—a statistical advance not available at the time of writing.

Summary

This chapter has presented a part of a piece of research which moves a key issue in Celtic language attitudes research from simple to more refined analyses. The original Celtic language attitude research tended to examine gender, age, language background, type of school attended and achievement in Welsh in terms of their separate connections with language attitudes. Using a sample of 797 children who were aged 11 to 14 at the beginning of the research, these variables were measured alongside the youth cultural affiliations and contexts chosen by the sample. Language attitudes were reduced to three scales : a general, traditional attitude scale, integrative attitudes and instrumental attitudes. All the variables were entered into overall models of the relationships between these variables.

The results presented in this chapter suggested that attitudes to Welsh were generally favourable. Favourable instrumental and integrative attitudes were found among 11 to 14 year olds. However, the Welsh language was regarded as unimportant for playing sport and watching TV and videos. This negative comment about Welsh may cause concern. Both contexts, sport and mass media, tend to be major items in many teenagers' lives. A particular critical age in teenagers' attitudes becoming less favourable is at 14 years of age, during the third year in secondary schooling. On a more positive note, involvement in traditional Welsh culture and books was connected with more favourable attitudes. Indeed, such cultural contexts appeared to have the most potent and influential effect on language attitudes. This hints that an essential support mechanism of a minority language under threat is the provision of attractive cultural activities (in the widest sense) for an age group where rapid personal and social changes occur.

4 Attitudes to Bilingualism

Introduction

This chapter examines the nature and attributes of attitude to bilingualism as different from attitude to a language. The concept of a holistic view of bilingualism is explored and tested. Two languages are capable of being seen within an individual and within society in terms of an entity and totality. Apart from a fractional view of two separate languages in bilingualism, an organic view is possible.

Previous research on attitude to languages has tended to keep languages apart. The research on attitude to Welsh, for example, has often utilised two separate language scales. Attitude to Welsh was often the principal interest with attitude to English added for comparison purposes. There has been no attitude to bilingualism scale, no scale where the focus is on two languages interacting together. Four items will illustrate the point. An attitude to Welsh scale may contain items such as found in Sharp *et al.* (1973):

> We should work hard to save the Welsh language.
> Welsh has no place in the modern world.

An English attitude scale may contain statements such as:

> English is one of the greatest languages in the world.
> We should leave it to the English to speak English.

These first two pairs of items reflect positive and negative attitudes to each language as a single entity. Each statement focuses upon one language out of context of the other language. In Sharp *et al.*'s (1973) Attitude to English scales, there are statements which include both languages, but in a negative and contrastive manner.

> I should not like English to take over from the Welsh language.
> English will take you further than Welsh.
> The Welsh language is better than the English language.
> English is easier to learn than Welsh.
> The Welsh ought to speak Welsh, not a second-hand language like English.
> One should not learn English too early in life, in case one is led to

disregard Welsh.

The English language is killing the Welsh language.

English books are better than Welsh books.

English should not be any more important than Welsh in Wales.

In each of the examples above, the underlying assumption is of competition, one language threatening the other. Positive consequences for one language imply negative consequences for the other language. This gives the impression of languages existing in a kind of balance. As one prospers, the other declines. This tends to suggest a deficiency model of bilingualism. The one increases at the expense of the other. As will be argued later, this is a subtractive view of bilingualism. Such a popular viewpoint does not present the whole story.

Similarly, in the measurement of integrative and instrumental attitudes (see Chapter 2), languages have been separated. For example, in Gardner & Lambert's (1972) seminal study there are items such as: '[French] will allow me to meet and converse with more and varied people', and 'I feel that no one is really educated unless he is fluent in the French language.'

One exception to the pattern of language attitudes research is Spina's (1979) Index of Bilingual Commitment. This is a five item scale, with the following 'integrated' view of bilingualism being represented in the first three items:

(1) French and English should be required in all Canadian schools.
(2) It would be a good thing if all Canadians could speak both English and French.
(3) It would be a good idea to have road signs printed in both English and French.
(4) There is no reason why an English-speaking Canadian should have to learn French if he is never going to use it.
(5) As far as I concerned, Canada should just have one official language.

The following set of items also illustrate the integrated viewpoint on bilingualism in terms of Welsh and English language statements:

Speaking both Welsh and English is important.

Speaking two languages is better than speaking one language.

Speaking two languages makes people cleverer.

Speaking both Welsh and English helps with finding employment.

Speaking both Welsh and English helps someone to benefit from two cultures.

It is important to be able to read in two languages. All schoolchildren should become fluent in English and Welsh.

You have more friends if you can speak English and Welsh.

The viewpoint of such items is that two languages can co-exist in a positive, helpful and mutually reciprocating beneficial manner. Rather than the image of a balance, the picture suggested is of building together. Addition rather than subtraction. Multiplication rather than division. One plus one making more than two; the product being greater than the mere sum of the components. There are assumptions in this viewpoint, assumptions about the possibility of harmonious co-existence at an individual or societal level, assumptions about positive and additive outcomes of a partnership between two languages. Not all agree with such assumptions. Saunders Lewis, for example, argued that bilingualism is a killer of the minority Welsh language.

François Grosjean (1985,1989) makes a strong argument for this additive, positive view of bilingualism. He outlines the monolingual or fractional view of bilingualism as opposed to the bilingual or holistic view. The fractional view is of the bilingual as two monolinguals in one person. The bilingual is viewed as having two isolated language competencies. This, Grosjean (1985,1989) argues, leads to discrediting bilinguals as being imbalanced in their language abilities (i.e. more competent at one language than another), to appraising the standards of bilinguals in monolingual terms, to questions about detrimental cognitive effects being hypothesised to occur with bilingualism rather than monolingualism, to viewing the language systems as autonomous and liable to interference, and to surveys of bilingualism carried out in terms of the two separate languages. Grosjean (1985) argues that 'it is important to stress how negative—often destructive—the monolingual view of bilingualism has been, and in many areas, still is' (p. 471).

Instead, Grosjean (1985,1989) argues that a different view should be taken of bilinguals. The holistic view suggests that we should not decompose into separate parts. Rather the view of bilingualism should be an integrated one. The bilingual is not two monolinguals in one frame, but a unity uniquely different from a monolingual. The frame of comparison requires moving from that of the monoglot to the bilingual. In the same way, to be bicultural is not to own two monocultures. The way two or more cultures are blended, harmonised and combined is unique and not simply the sum of two parts.

Grosjean (1985,1989) suggests that we should no longer ask the simple question about whether a bilingual has developed the language competency of monolinguals. The bilingual tends to use different languages in differing contexts, with different people. 'Because the needs and uses of the two languages are usually quite different, the bilingual is rarely equally or completely fluent in the two languages ..... Because the bilingual is a human communicator (as is the monolingual), he or she has developed a communicative competence that is sufficient for everyday life' (Grosjean, 1985: 471-2). Thus measurement of a bilingual's competence can only be achieved by examining total language repertoire enacted in varying domains. Measurement needs to study the bilingual as a whole, which means that one language cannot be measured without measuring the other. No profile or test score should exist without portraying bilingual competences. Single language scores deny the fullness and wholeness of a bilingual's language skills. Monolingual standards become inappropriate points of comparison in the holistic viewpoint about bilingualism.

In terms of this chapter, the focus is on attitudes to bilingualism, particularly from an integrated, holistic viewpoint. Such a focus is promoted by examining four issues:

(1) What is attitude to bilingualism and how may it be measured?
(2) The development of a measuring device for attitude to bilingualism.
(3) Is attitude to bilingualism, within the conceptions of a sample of teenagers, different from attitude to a specific language.
(4) What kind of relationships does attitude to bilingualism exhibit with other personal characteristics and attributes.

The Characterisation of Attitude to Bilingualism

The previous section sought to sketch the notion of a holistic view of bilingualism. This section narrows the focus to attitude to bilingualism. Attitude to bilingualism concerns the viewpoint that languages can be fused or can exist in tandem. Such attitudes may be positive or negative towards this concept. An example may illustrate the initial hypothesis that attitude to bilingualism can be conceptually distinct from attitude to a specific language. Take two statements:

The English language is killing the Welsh language.
Children in Wales should learn to read both English and Welsh.

The first statement sets one language against the other. This represents the decomposed, fractional view of two languages. The second statement does not represent an alternative or preference. In this second statement, there may be an additive, bilateral viewpoint. The co-existence of two languages and their synchronisation (or lack of) is highlighted. Whether such a difference exists within the constructions of individuals needs to be tested. For the moment a hypothesis is made that there is a 'co-existence' view of bilingualism, as different from a 'separatist' viewpoint.

To test the hypothesis, an original 25 item attitude scale was developed over a period of time. Neither Spina's (1979) Index of Bilingual Commitment nor the Attitude to Bilingual Education Scale (Lewis, Rado & Foster, 1982) provided an appropriate set of attitude items. Inspection of the items provides a characterisation of attitude to bilingualism.

(1) It is important to be able to speak English and Welsh.
(2) To speak one language in Wales is all that is needed.
(3) Knowing Welsh and English makes people cleverer.
(4) Children get confused when learning English and Welsh.
(5) Speaking both Welsh and English helps to get a job.
(6) Being able to write in English and Welsh is important.
(7) All schools in Wales should teach pupils to speak in Welsh and English.
(8) Road signs should be in English and Welsh.
(9) Speaking two languages is not difficult.
(10) Knowing both Welsh and English gives people problems.
(11) I feel sorry for people who cannot speak both English and Welsh.
(12) Children in Wales should learn to read in both Welsh and English.
(13) People know more if they speak English and Welsh.
(14) People who speak Welsh and English can have more friends than those who speak one language.
(15) Speaking both English and Welsh is more for older than younger people.
(16) Speaking both Welsh and English helps people get promotion in their job.
(17) Young children learn to speak Welsh and English at the same time with ease.
(18) Both English and Welsh should be important in Wales.
(19) People can earn more money if they speak both Welsh and English.
(20) I should not like English to take over from the Welsh language.
(21) When I become an adult, I would like to be considered as a speaker of English and Welsh.
(22) All people in Wales should speak Welsh and English.
(23) If I have children, I would want them to speak both English and Welsh.
(24) Both the Welsh and English languages can live together in Wales.
(25) People only need to know one language.

The twenty-five items need to be regarded as the initial pool to be refined by a latent variable analysis. Refinement often means that items outside of most respondents' range of experience (often answered as the ambiguous 'neither agree nor disagree' response) will be located. Similarly, conceptually idiosyncratic or unique items may be uncovered. For example, item 20 (I should not like English to take over from the Welsh language) may be 'language in conflict' rather than a 'holistic bilingual' item.

The Development of an Attitude to Bilingualism Scale

The 25 item scale was given to the 797 teenagers (described in Chapter 2). Before looking at which items proved to be valid or not, an initial viewing of how the teenagers responded is valuable. This indicates the dominant viewpoints of the sample. Details are given in the following table. The respondents were invited to give one of five responses to each item:

Strongly Agree	SA
Agree	A
Neither Agree Nor Disagree	NAND
Disagree	D
Strongly Disagree	SD

Table 4.1 Frequencies of response to attitude to bilingualism items

	SD %	D %	NAND %	A %	SA %
1. It is important to be able to speak English and Welsh	2.0	7.3	15.8	45.4	29.4
2. To speak one language in Wales is all that is needed	9.6	34.6	32.5	17.3	6.0
3. Knowing Welsh and English makes people cleverer	4.7	17.2	27.2	38.8	12.1
4. Children get confused when learning English and Welsh	13.3	35.5	21.1	22.2	7.9
5. Speaking both Welsh and English helps to get a job	1.1	3.7	9.8	48.3	37.0
6. Being able to write in English and Welsh is important	2.3	6.5	19.1	44.3	27.8
7. All schools in Wales should teach pupils to speak in Welsh and English	2.3	8.2	16.3	40.3	32.8
8. Road signs should be in English & Welsh	3.1	8.0	18.3	43.9	26.6
9. Speaking two languages is not difficult	5.9	14.2	19.1	41.7	19.1
10. Knowing both Welsh and English gives people problems	15.3	45.8	26.3	9.7	2.9

11. I feel sorry for people who cannot speak both English and Welsh	9.5	22.8	32.5	25.1	10.1
12. Children in Wales should learn to read in Welsh and English	3.1	9.8	19.3	45.0	22.8
13. People know more if they speak English and Welsh	3.4	13.5	26.5	40.6	15.9
14. People who speak Welsh and English can have more friends than those who speak one language	14.6	21.6	27.2	24.1	12.5
15. Speaking both English and Welsh is more for older than younger people	9.3	21.5	31.3	27.6	10.2
16. Speaking both Welsh and English should help people get promotion in their job	3.1	9.8	23.3	44.0	19.8
17. Young children learn to speak Welsh and English at the same time with ease	4.5	21.3	35.9	29.3	8.9
18. Both English and Welsh should be important in Wales	3.3	6.8	18.9	49.4	21.5
19. People can earn more money if they speak both Welsh and English	8.6	19.4	31.5	29.3	11.2
20. I should not like English to take over from the Welsh language	8.3	10.2	22.5	24.4	34.7
21. When I become an adult, I would like to be considered as a speaker of English and Welsh	4.0	10.0	23.8	38.5	23.6
22. All people in Wales should speak Welsh and English	5.2	16.8	28.2	33.9	15.8
23. If I have children, I would want them to speak both English and Welsh	4.5	10.5	19.2	40.1	25.7
24. Both the Welsh and English language can live together in Wales	4.4	5.2	21.9	46.2	22.3
25. People only need to know one language	19.6	32.2	28.0	14.3	5.9

Table 4.1 suggests two things. First, the dominant attitude is one of favourability towards bilingualism. There is a definite degree of positiveness towards bilingualism in Wales. Bilingualism is seen as pragmatic

in terms of individual ownership (cognition), education and wider society. It is also seen as advantageous in affiliative, cultural and utilitarian contexts. Second, the pupils found little or no difficulty in answering the questions. On most items, there is a spread of scores across the five answer categories and a swing to one direction. The 'Neither Agree nor Disagree Category', sometimes used as a bucket for ambiguous, irrelevant or difficult items (as well as for neutral opinions), is not prominently used with any item. This suggests that the attitude scale was comprehensive and appropriate for the 11 to 14 year olds. This also hints that a modified version might well be suitable for adults. Further, the number of 'missing' responses for each item was few. On average less than 1 person in a 100 accidentally or deliberately left an item blank. This is another indicator of the feasibility of the scale.

The next stage in constructing the scale was to submit the 25 items to a latent variable analysis. Details of the procedure used may be found in Appendix 2. Since individual items tend, by themselves, to be unreliable when used to judge attitudes, a combination of items is normally required. Latent variable analysis both helps locate the more central items in a scale, and also detects whether the items are best allocated to one or more scales. The Scree test (see Appendix 2) to determine the number of latent variables to extract was slightly ambiguous and suggested the possibility of one or two groups of items. For reasons of interpretability and internal reliability, one grouping was clearly preferable. The one grouping of items gave an alpha reliability of 0.89 across the 25 items.

Not all items were found to be equally weighted on the one latent variable. Figure 18 provides details of these loadings, ordered in descending size of weighting.

The five items most central to the scale are as follows:

Wanting children to speak English and Welsh (No. 23)
The importance of being able to write in English and Welsh (No. 6)
Children in Wales learning to read in both Welsh and English (No. 12)
The importance of being able to speak English and Welsh (No. 1)
Schools teaching pupils to speak in English and Welsh (No. 7)

Four items had loadings below 0.30 (Nos 2, 10, 15 and 24), and could be excluded from future uses of the scale without affecting internal reliability. If a scale with a small number of items is required, the twelve or more items with the highest latent variable loadings is unlikely to affect internal reliability.

The scale now requires two tests. First, does the scale maintain its integrity when placed against items from the other language attitude scales? That is, if the 25 items are entered into a latent variable analysis

alongside a large number of items from other language scales, does attitude
to bilingualism stay distinct? Second, does the attitude to bilingualism scale
begin to demonstrate some validity when related to other key variables in
the research? Is the attitude to bilingualism scale a good predictor or
correlate of other entities measured in the research? It is to these two issues,
the chapter now turns.

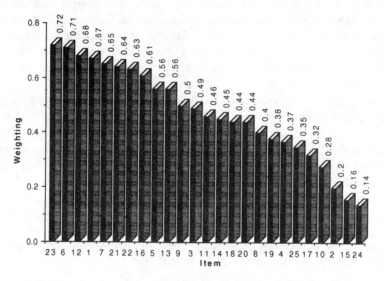

Figure 4.1

The Uniqueness of Attitude to Bilingualism

Sixty-five items were entered into an overall latent variable analysis.
Twenty-five items from the attitude to bilingualism questionnaire were
added to 40 items measuring attitude to the Welsh language and uses of
the Welsh language (Parts Three and Four of the questionnaire—see
Appendix 1). The overall latent variable analysis puts the uniqueness of
the attitude to bilingualism scale to a crucial examination. Ideally the great
majority of the 25 items believed to represent attitude to bilingualism will
be kept apart from the other Welsh language items. When all 65 items were
entered into the melting pot, the hope was that one grouping of items
would clearly and unambiguously represent attitude to bilingualism.

In the style of a confirmatory latent variable analysis, three groupings
were extracted. The hypothesis was that the three latent variables would
represent the three different questionnaires: attitude to bilingualism, atti-

tude to the Welsh language and the uses and value of Welsh (integrative and instrumental attitudes).

Table 4.2 provides results from this latent variable analysis. The table is separated into three parts, showing how distinctly the three sets of items are reproduced by the latent variable analysis. Simply stated, the research sample latently appear to conceive of attitude to bilingualism as distinctly different from attitude to the Welsh language, and as distinct from the uses and value of Welsh. Attitude to Bilingualism appears conceptually apart from attitude to a single language.

Table 4.2 The weightings of the three latent variables

Questionnaire: The Uses and Value of Welsh (integrative and instrumental attitudes)

	Latent Variable 1	Latent Variable 2	Latent Variable 3
Item 1		0.69	
Item 2		0.46	
Item 3		0.61	
Item 4		0.64	
Item 5		0.48	
Item 6		0.50	
Item 7		0.56	
Item 8		0.72	
Item 9	0.44		
Item10	0.43	-0.51	
Item11	0.48	-0.35	
Item12		0.66	
Item13		-0.59	
Item14		0.55	
Item15		-0.58	
Item16		0.56	
Item17		0.61	
Item18		0.72	
Item19	0.40	-0.52	
Item20		0.67	

(All loadings below 0.40 on the first latent variable, below 0.35 on the second latent variable, and below 0.30 on the third latent variable are left blank).

Questionnaire: General Attitude to the Welsh Language

	Latent Variable 1	Latent Variable 2	Latent Variable 3
Item 1	0.72		
Item2	-0.55		
Item3	0.44		
Item4	-0.43		
Item5	0.73		
Item6			
Item7	-0.43		
Item8	0.72		
Item9	0.69		
Item10	0.64		
Item11			
Item12	0.67		
Item14	0.52		
Item15	0.77		
Item16			
Item17			
Item18	0.81		
Item19	0.71		
Item20	0.78		

Questionnaire: Attitude to Bilingualism

	Latent Variable 1	Latent Variable 2	Latent Variable 3
Item 1			0.51
Item2			-0.30
Item3			0.40
Item4	-0.40		
Item5			0.53
Item6	0.45		0.52
Item7			0.52

Item8		
Item9	0.47	
Item10		
Item11		
Item12	0.51	0.43
Item13		0.41
Item14		0.31
Item15		
Item16		0.54
Item17		
Item18		0.56
Item19		0.43
Item20	0.49	
Item21	0.40	0.46
Item22		0.54
Item23	0.46	0.53
Item24		0.35
Item25		-0.34

Latent variable one in Table 4.2 reproduces the general attitude to the Welsh Language dimension. Of the 20 items from the questionnaire designed to measure attitude to the Welsh language, only three obtained loadings under 0.40 on the first latent variable. Latent variable two reproduces the values and uses of the Welsh Language scale (integrative and instrumental). Only one item from the 20 items in the original scale was excluded by the latent variable analysis. On this overall latent variable analysis, the distinction between integrative and instrumental attitudes was not reproduced. The separation of this latent variable from a general attitude to Welsh latent variable is clear. Seven of the items from the 25 item Attitude to Bilingualism questionnaire were placed on the first latent variable. This suggests that there may be some small overlap between Attitude to Bilingualism and Attitude to the Welsh language.

Latent variable three contains 17 items which load over 0.30. All 17 items come from the Attitude to Bilingualism questionnaire. No items from the other two questionnaires were present on latent variable three. Eight of the 25 original items on the Attitude to Bilingualism questionnaire did not attain loadings high enough (0.30) to be included on that latent variable. However, the result is clearly that Attitude to Bilingualism is defined as conceptually distinct to attitude to a single language. It therefore seems to be a measurable indicator of language attitudes and is separate from the traditional conceptualisation of attitudes to a single language. This scale can be further examined by testing for relationships with other important variables.

The Utility of Attitude to Bilingualism

The research sample used to produce the Attitude to Bilingualism scale also provided data on a defined range of individual differences and contextual variations (see Chapter 3). For example, data on gender and age represents individual differences; data on school and language background represents the context in which individual differences are enacted. Attitude to Bilingualism is now examined in terms of its relationships to these differences. These variables are later brought together into one overall analysis.

The initial questions to be answered by the research may be simply stated as: Who has more favourable attitudes to bilingualism? Females or Males? Younger Teenagers or Older Teenagers? Higher or Lower Ability pupils? Following these, a particular concern is how different profiles on youth culture relate to attitude to bilingualism.

First, with respect to gender, no differences were found between males and females. While females had slightly the more positive attitude to bilingualism, this did not reach customary levels of statistical significance. Second, age was related to attitude to bilingualism. The younger pupils in the sample tended to have the more favourable attitudes. For example, the average 11 year old scored 53.79 (a latent variable score expressed as a 'T' score—with a mean of 50 and a standard deviation of 10), while the average 14 year old scored 48.04. Analysis showed that the only statistically significant difference was between the under 14 year olds and the 14 year olds ($p = 0.0001$).

The age difference in attitude to bilingualism suggests two related issues. First, a pattern similar to attitude to minority languages may be present. As reviewed in Chapter 3, attitude to Welsh, for example, becomes less favourable with advancing age. So with attitude to bilingualism, there is the possibility of a decline in positiveness with age. Second, the decline is not necessarily linear. It is not simply the case that with each succeeding year, attitude declines in favourability. The result suggest that between 13 and 14 years of age there is a particular drop. As children move through the third year in secondary school, favourability of attitude to bilingualism appears to decline markedly.

The third result concerns ability. This variable was also statistically significant ($p= 0.001$) in its relationship with attitude to bilingualism. Those who rated themselves as above average ability in Welsh tended to have a more favourable attitude to bilingualism. The lower the perceived ability in Welsh, the less favourable the attitude to bilingualism.

The fourth result concerns youth culture. The youth culture questionnaire produced two latent variables, termed Welsh Traditional and Literary Culture and Popular Culture (see Chapter 3). Those scoring highly on the first latent variable spend time in Eisteddfodau, Yr Urdd, Church or Chapel and reading books out of school and going to the Library. The first latent variable joins both a Welsh and a literary culture. The second youth culture latent variable contained items concerned with gregariousness and mass media orientation. Pupils scoring highly on this latent variable spend much of their time with boyfriends and girlfriends, going to discos, listening to records and cassettes, watching TV and videos and going shopping.

The relationship between these two youth culture latent variables and attitude to Bilingualism is summed up in two correlations. Between Welsh traditional & literary culture and Attitude to Bilingualism the correlation was 0.37. This shows a definite, moderate connection. Those who have more favourable attitudes to Bilingualism tend to engage more in Welsh cultural and literary forms. The second correlation is small and weak (-0.08). The relationship between attitude to Bilingualism and popular youth culture is statistically significant ($p=0.02$), but meagre and tenuous. The slight trend is for those who engage more in 'pop' culture to be less favourable in their attitude to bilingualism.

Apart from differences between individuals, a further source of validity for the attitude to bilingualism scale is found in its relationship to the contexts which may affect groups of people other than youth culture: the school attended by the pupil, and the language background of the pupil. Both these context variables are not normally chosen by the individual.

Three secondary schools (11–18) used in the research represent different types of school in Wales. The first is a school in a Welsh heartland area. This has been termed a Natural Welsh school (see Chapter 3). The second is a school in an anglicised area and the designation of the school is as a Designated Bilingual School ('Ysgolion Cymraeg'). That is, it operates in Welsh throughout most of the curriculum. The third school is also in an Anglicised area where less than 10% of the population speak Welsh. The school operates almost solely through the medium of English.

The comparison of the three schools on the Attitude to Bilingualism scale located a considerable difference. The highest mean score was gained by the Designated Bilingual School (54.12). The lowest mean was found in the English medium school (44.64). Significantly different from the other two schools, and in the middle, was the natural Welsh school with a mean of 52.17.

The result is intriguing. It is children from a relatively more Anglicised environment , taking their education in a Welsh-medium environment, who are most favourable to bilingualism. Those from a relatively more Welsh language environment, while being more positive towards bilingualism than the English-medium pupils, were nevertheless distinctly less favourable than those in the designated bilingual secondary school. This is made more intriguing when set against another analysis. When comparing the designated bilingual secondary school with the natural Welsh school on Attitude to the Welsh Language, no statistically significant difference was found. So attitude to bilingualism does not become more favourable in line with attitude to Welsh becoming less favourable. Indeed the designated bilingual secondary school had a more (but a statistically insignificant) favourable attitude to Welsh mean score (54.15) than the natural Welsh school (53.70). Attitude to Welsh does not become less positive when someone holds a favourable attitude to bilingualism. The same pattern was found with the Integrative and Instrumental Attitude to Welsh latent variables.

A positive orientation to bilingualism is found in a school where most children are from Welsh homes in a predominantly English speaking community. They appear to celebrate the idea of bilingualism rather than polarise towards or against the Welsh language. The question which arises is the origins of such an attitude. Is the school itself a principal effect on a favourable attitude to bilingualism? Or does the influence come more from the family? What effect does the local environment have on the pupil? What is the relationship and interaction between school, family and community in influencing attitude to bilingualism? The level of consciousness about bilingualism may be stronger where Welsh speakers are in an Anglicised environment. Bilingualism may be more prominent, more necessary, more noticed where Welsh speakers form patchy pools in an expanse of anglophone language and culture. The level of consciousness about bilingualism may also be stronger in a designated bilingual school due to its situation, aims and operation.

More light may be thrown on the relationship between school and attitude to bilingualism by two analyses: first, by looking at the effect of language background on all pupils (and then specifically in interaction with type of school attended); second, by putting language background, school and the individual difference variables into an equation to calculate major and minor effects.

Language background was measured by a latent variable analysis weighted 21 item scale. The correlation between attitude to bilingualism and language background was 0.46, indicating that the more Welsh language the background of the person, the more favourable attitude they showed to bilingualism. Given the previous analysis rega rding differences between schools, this link between language background and attitude to bilingualism seems capable of elaboration. The initial interest is whether there is any difference between the four language background groups on attitude to bilingualism. Table 4.3 provides the details.

Table 4.3 Language background compared with attitude to bilingualism

Group	Mean Score on Attitude to Bilingualism
Welsh dominant	55.48
Bilingual/Welsh bias	54.19
Bilingual/English bias	52.96
English dominant	44.62
	$(p = 0.00001)$

The finding is that the major difference lies between the English dominant group compared with the Bilingual and Welsh groups combined. The English dominant group has the least favourable attitude to bilingualism, while the other three groups all score well above the overall average (50.00). The pattern is not a simple linear one. That is, it is not the case that the more Welsh the language background, the more positive the attitude to bilingualism. There is an apparent steep rise in favourability of attitude stemming from an English language background to the bilingual language background continuum. The gradient between having a bilingual language background and a Welsh dominant background is small (and statistically insignificant).

Having found that the designated bilingual secondary school tended to show more favourable attitudes to bilingualism, it is now important to look for any interaction between language background and type of school. Such an analysis looks, for example, at whether pupils from more English language backgrounds have different attitudes to bilingualism if they attend a designated bilingual secondary school or a natural Welsh school. Such an analysis also goes some way towards deciphering the extent of effects on attitude to bilingualism when language background is set against school. Which of these two contextual variables appear more important? (This issue is examined more fully in the next section).

Table 4.4 provides a breakdown of mean scores on attitude to bilingualism when school and language background are both considered.

Table 4.4 School, language background and attitude to bilingualism

	School		
	Natural Welsh	*Designated Bilingual*	*English Medium*
Language Group			
Welsh dominant	56.49	54.79	-
Bilingual/Welsh bias	53.17	55.58	-
Bilingual/English bias	51.49	53.74	-
English dominant	45.20	-	44.64

Notes: (i) Significance of Interaction by 2 way ANOVA = 0.08. (ii) A dash (-) indicates too few numbers within a cell for a generalisable mean. The four absent means had less than 4 pupils.

The table suggests a marginally significant ($p = 0.08$) difference between the natural Welsh school and the designated bilingual secondary school. Pupils from the designated bilingual secondary school tend to have comparatively similar attitude to bilingualism scores, irrespective of having a more Welsh or a more English background. Children from the natural Welsh school tend, in contrast, to vary more with language background. In that school, the more Welsh the background, the more favourable the attitude to bilingualism. This possible influence of school on children is highlighted in comparing children from similar language backgrounds. In the two bilingual groups, pupils in the designated bilingual secondary school have a slightly more favourable attitude to bilingualism. This hints at an effect of school over and above that of language background. At the same time, within the 'dominant Welsh' language background group, the natural Welsh school has marginally a higher mean. This tends to confirm and extend a previous finding, that attitude to bilingualism is enhanced and not detracted by a strong Welsh language environment. Attitude to the Welsh language was found to be positively related to attitude to bilingualism. Here, external characteristics, language background and school, both positively relate 'Welshness' and attitude to bilingualism.

A Model of Attitude to Bilingualism

In previous sections, relationships between age, gender, ability, youth culture, language background, school and attitude to bilingualism have been examined. The key issue which arises must be 'which of these char-

acteristics is most influential?' Is youth culture, for example, more powerful in influencing attitude to bilingualism than language background?

There are two ways in which this can be achieved. Firstly, by examining
the correlations of each variable with attitude to bilingualism. Secondly,
by constructing a causal model of attitude to bilingualism.

Initial relationships with attitude to bilingualism

The size of the correlation coefficient between attitude to bilingualism
and the other variables provides an initial glimpse of major and minor
effects. These are listed in Table 4.5.

Table 4.5 Correlation with attitude to bilingualism

Gender	0.05 (p = n.s.)
Age	-0.14 (p = 0.0001)
Ability (Welsh)	0.30 (p = 0.0001)
Youth Culture I (Welsh/Literary)	0.37 (p = 0.0001)
Youth Culture II ('Popular')	-0.08 (p = 0.04)
School (English Vs. Welsh Medium)	0.30 (p = 0.001)
Language Background	0.45 (p = 0.0001)

Note: The School correlation represents the English medium school compared with the
other two schools combined.

The list of correlations suggest language background as the single most
important effect on attitude to bilingualism. Language background is
followed by a group of three correlations in the 0.3 range, namely Welsh
and Literary Youth Culture, School and Ability in Welsh. Well below that
group comes age and 'popular' culture, with gender an insignificant
influence.

The ordering indicates that it is not personality characteristics that are
dominant. Rather it is the environment that is more influential—the language of the home, street, school and mass media, the ties with eisteddfodau and Yr Urdd (Welsh League of Youth). Not only do situational
variables seem more important in links with attitude to bilingualism, but
there is the notion of such attitudes being part of social norms and values.
Such attitudes may be part of an ideology that is open to change by altered
environments.

A model of relationships with attitude to bilingualism

A more sophisticated way of dealing with relationships between individual and context variables and attitude to bilingualism is to compose a

testable model of causes and effects (see Figure 4.2). A model was constructed using variables considered in this chapter. Such a model, informed
by the results of Chapter 3, provides an hypothesis to be tested. It is partly
rooted in the input–context–output model (see Baker, 1985; Baker, 1988).
There are three stages. First, gender, school, age and language background
form relatively fixed inputs. That is, they are not chosen by the pupil (with
some small exceptions in school and language background). The second
stage concerns chosen contexts, namely the two youth culture latent variables. Pupils have a certain degree of choice over their engagement in
youth culture. The third stage represents attitude to bilingualism and
ability in Welsh. These may be viewed as outputs or outcomes of the causal
process.

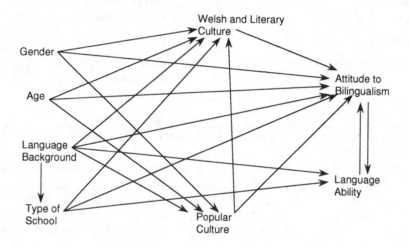

Figure 4.2 Initial model for testing

In this hypothetical model for testing, each of the fixed inputs is related
directly and indirectly to attitude to bilingualism. The indirect paths
mostly operate through the two youth culture variables. Attitude and
ability are examined for mutual interaction. Added to this model was the
reliabilities of the latent variable scales. Appendix 2 provides a description
and explanation of the analysis of the model by LISREL.

The final model following testing and modification is represented in the
following simplified diagram (Figure 4.3). Appendix 2 provides a fuller
representation of the process, the disturbance terms and the statistics of the
final model.

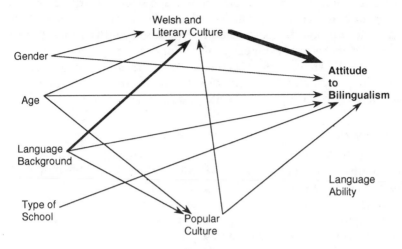

Figure 4.3

Note: The model shows the paths with coefficients over 0.25. The thickness of the arrows represent the strength of the association.

In terms of direct paths, Welsh and literary youth culture has the largest effect on attitude to bilingualism. More minor direct effects are exhibited by language background, gender, age, school and Popular culture. A strong indirect effect stems from language background, in terms of its influence particularly on Welsh and literary culture, but also on Popular culture. Ability in Welsh and type of school attended have only small effects (see Appendix 2 for the full model). The determination of total and indirect effects confirms and expands the analysis (see Table 4.6)

Table 4.6 Summary of effects on attitude to bilingualism

	Total	Indirect
Gender	0.02	0.28
Age	-0.10	-0.37
Language Background	0.50	0.86
Welsh and Literary Youth Culture	0.998	0.02
Popular Culture	0.02	0.27
School	0.21	-0.07
Ability in Welsh	0.17	n/a

Table 4.6 suggests that it is Welsh and literary youth culture which has the greatest effect on attitude to bilingualism, with language background in second place. School and ability in Welsh have a definite but smaller

direct effect. Popular culture, gender and age have little direct effect on attitude to bilingualism. A consideration of indirect effects reveals that gender and age have distinct effects on attitude via youth culture. The most marked indirect effect is language background, particularly in its effect on attitude via Welsh and Literary culture. As in the models in the previous chapter, popular culture has an indirect effect on attitude to bilingualism by influencing participation in Welsh and Literary activities.

Conclusions

The conclusion would seem to be that attitude to bilingualism is related to the youth culture of teenage years and relatively less related to institutions such as the family and school. Individual attributes such as gender, age, even ability in Welsh also seem to exhibit a more minor influence. 'Popular' culture appears to have a moderate negative influence while language background has a moderate positive influence.

This analysis highlights the importance of youth culture as a determinant of attitude to bilingualism. While home and school are clearly of some influence, the more major influence is with peers and 'Popular' culture, engaging in Welsh cultural forms such as Yr Urdd and eisteddfodau, reading and visiting the library. The drama of the socialisation process of the teenage years, acted out on different chosen cultural stages and in varying theatres, seems highly influential in the production of attitudes to bilingualism.

5 Language and Attitude Change

Introduction

It is an implicit or explicit assumption of much language policy and provision that attitudes can or should change. For example, one outcome of bilingual education may be a favourable attitude to a second language or a heritage minority language. The recent considerable expansion in the teaching of Welsh to adults in Wales by Ulpans, evening classes and summer schools presumably aims to influence attitudes to the Welsh language and culture in addition to teaching language skills. In a 'melting pot' or transitional-assimilationist language context (e.g. in-migrants mastering English), engendering positive attitudes to the majority tongue and culture is often a covert part of the transitional programme.

Where a language is fighting for survival, encouraging positive attitudes becomes crucial. As E.G. Lewis (1981) asserts, 'in some instances a language policy is in fact largely if not principally concerned with inculcating attitudes either to the languages or to the speakers of those languages' (p. 262). Attitudes change over time—rarely are they static. The reasons for change is the subject of this chapter. However, before proceeding, it is important to note that attitude change in a language context has a strong political dimension. While this chapter will concentrate mostly on the social psychological explanation of language change, it is clear that language attitudes are manipulated by power groups. Such manipulation can be by gentle persuasion, intensive indoctrination, subtle influence or Machiavellian programming. Attitudes to language may change by slow evolution and gradual development. They can also take 'U' turns parallel with sudden religious conversion. Language attitudes may change due to internal thinking; more often they change by exposure to social influence.

Historical Perspective

For those interested in language attitude change, one danger is to focus solely on a present, person-oriented perspective or contemporary sociopolitical perspective. It is perhaps salutary and important to take an historical perspective. Such a perspective may start from a portrayal of how much language attitudes have changed over a century or more. The historian may be able to explore and evaluate the historical causes of language attitude change. By examining ideology and institution, power and prestige, conflicts and class, figureheads and fashions, important factors in historical change may be teased out. The description of historical attitude change, and the analytical evaluation and interpretation of causes of change, are rarely examined by social psychological theorists nor sociolinguists. However such an historical approach (properly by sociological or social historians, e.g. H.G. Williams, 1978), is a vital foundation in the study of language change.

A brief illustration of language attitude change in an historical perspective is that of the Welsh language. The day schools of the nineteenth century attempted to suppress the use of Welsh in education. 'It was the declared aim of these schools to make Welsh children proficient in the English tongue and to dismiss the use of Welsh. British and National schools would boast that they taught all subjects through the medium of English, and the same was true of voluntaryist and works schools' (B.L. Davies, 1988: 133). Simply stated, in much of the nineteenth century and the early decades of the twentieth century, strong attitudes to the utilitarian value of English were prominent in education. By the 1970s and 1980s a reversal in attitudes in the county of Gwynedd has occurred. Welsh is regarded as having utilitarian value, being a condition of many jobs. From a nineteenth century attitude of English being the road to success and prosperity, in certain parts of Wales, the attitude has changed to Welsh as opening doors to careers and capital (Williams, 1986).

Similarly, attitudes to Welsh as a teaching medium have changed. From a nineteenth century exclusion of Welsh from almost all of the curriculum, the indigenous language has become a medium of curriculum communication in all school subjects. As Baker (1990a) considered, the growth of Welsh medium schools, the increase in examinations and examination entrants taking subjects through the medium of Welsh has risen constantly since the early 1950s. More children are becoming fluent in Welsh at primary school level, and the exponential rise in adult classes learning Welsh and in pre-school Welsh medium playgroups, is evidence of a 'U' turn in attitudes to Welsh in this century.

Why attitudes have changed so dramatically this century has yet to be thoroughly explored. Developments in mass communications, transport, industrialisation, urbanisation and in-migration are all potential threats to the Welsh language. Perhaps attitudes have changed as a reaction to the anglicising influences of such twentieth century developments. The penetration of English language television, films, videos and music into homes, and concerns about the linguistic imbalance of heartland Welsh communities when faced with monolingual in-migrants, appear to have produced a backlash in terms of an increased consciousness regarding the decline of the indigenous language. Such an increase of awareness appears to have permeated Welsh speakers, those who are Welsh but do not speak Welsh, and English monolingual in-migrants. Such a pattern is just one possible cause of changing attitudes, and is given as an illustration of how an historical analysis is a most important complementary approach to attitude change alongside social psychological approaches. An historical–sociological account of attitude change is a vital parallel approach to attitude change theory. The former will concentrate on causes of societal attitude change while the latter will focus more on individual and small group change. Both perspectives are important if we are to understand the causes of language attitude change. Sociolinguistic, political and geolinguistic explanations are also of importance in understanding attitude change.

This chapter proceeds by examining key social psychological theories of attitude change. Each of these theories has something different to contribute to an understanding of language attitude change.

Theories of Attitude Change

Functional theory

Katz (1960) provides four functions for an individual's attitudes. The four functions have important implications for attitude change.

The utilitarian or instrumental function

Attitudes may change when there is some reward. Acquisition of a minority language, using and maintaining a language or acquiring a positive attitude to that language may depend on gaining reward and avoiding punishment.

For example, the Irish CILAR research showed that approximately half the national sample believed that 'there is too much punishment associated with Irish in schools'. In Wales, the 'Welsh Not' was a very severe method of attitude change. Any child, during much of the nineteenth century, heard using Welsh in school was required to wear a wooden halter around their neck. When another child was heard speaking Welsh, the halter was transferred to that child. At the end of the school day, whoever was wearing the halter was beaten. Rewards in school for speaking a minority language may be more subtle: praise and encouragement from the teacher, more attention, more eye-contact, more interaction with the teacher. A language learnt in school needs encouragement and reinforcement outside. In Wales, Yr Urdd (the Welsh League of Youth) exists to foster a wide range of popular and traditional cultural activities through the medium of Welsh.

Having left school, adults need rewards to use a minority language. One example would be employment prospects which utilise or allow minority language usage. For minority language speech events to become more frequent, some tangible, social or individual reward system preferably needs to exist. Minority language television, discos, pop music, novels, papers, concerts, for example, all provide the stage upon which the prestige and status of a language is viewed and acted out. Such status and prestige supply and control the rewards and reinforcement for speaking a minority language. Where everyday events of perceived high status are almost entirely in the majority language, there may be little hope of attitude change. Attitude change can be made more probable when rewards can be gained and punishment avoided for speaking a minority language. Such punishment may be latent and barely obvious: the raising of a friend's eyelids in speaking Irish in public; being given less attention in shops when speaking Gaelic in Scotland; speaking Welsh when the disco music is North American and English.

Providing appropriate rewards for minority language activity depends on identifying what is perceived by the pupil or the employee as a reward. Praise for speaking a second language may work well with young children, but have the opposite effects to that intended if delivered by a teacher to a delinquent older pupil.

The ego defensive function

Basic inner security is essential for psychological health. People who hold attitudes which lead to insecurity, embarrassment and anxiety are likely to change their attitudes to achieve greater security and less anxiety. Speaking a minority language in a majority environment may lead to such anxiety. Being a peripheral member of a group, not sharing the common threads of identity of a group, lacking some of the status attributes of a reference group may lead to attitude and behavioural change. Majority group members sometimes defend their egos by denigrating a minority language. Fearing minority language groups being given privileges or greater worth, majority groups may hold negative attitudes towards such minorities to enhance their own self- worth and distinctiveness. Attitude change strategies therefore need to ensure ego defence mechanisms are either enhanced (e.g. by adding to self-esteem) or are not threatened nor attacked. Threats need to be removed, or catharsis needs to occur, or an individual needs to develop more self-insight (Katz, 1960).

Value-expressive function

Katz (1960) suggested that attitudes are expressed and activated when they are congruent with personal values and the self concept. Those who value Welsh cultural forms or who regard themselves as being very Welsh, whose core self identity is Welsh rather than English, may express attitudes logically emanating from such values. For minority language attitudes to become more favourable, it is evident that deep rooted personality characteristics need to be considered (Herman, 1968). The psychological notion of self concept, the picture we hold of ourself, may be a powerful governor of attitude change. When, for example, self concept in adolescence moves towards conformity with peer group identity, the peer group may become an important determinant of change towards, or away from, minority language and cultural identification. If social comparison occurs with majority cultural forms (e.g. the Anglo-American pop culture), then self concept and attitudes may change accordingly. If the social comparison process occurs with indigenous cultural forms, minority language and culture may be more open to positive attitude change.

Attitudes do not exist in a vacuum. They are part of an individual's whole psychological functioning (Bain & Yu, 1984). An individual with certain personality characteristics may be more or less open to attitude change.

Knowledge function

As expressed when considering attitude theory in Chapter 1, an attitude is said to have a cognitive or knowledge component. Attitudes facilitate understanding of people and events. Katz (1960) contended that attitudes are more susceptible to change when the knowledge function is known and understood. For example, adolescents for whom knowledge of Anglo-American popular music is necessary in order to gain peer status or to conform to group norms, will be likely to have, or change to, attitudes congruent with popular culture and their peer group.

Knowledge of minority or majority culture, social organisation, politics and education, for example, can affect attitude. In this sense knowledge precedes attitude, and helps explain attitude. Knowledge that participating in a Welsh male voice choir, a Scottish dance party, or in Irish folk music is invigorating, rewarding and enjoyable helps form or change an attitude.

Classical conditioning

Attitudes towards stimuli may become more favourable if they are associated with pleasant events. This is the essence of Pavlovian or classical conditioning. A simple experiment will illustrate. In Staats & Staats (1958) study, positive words such as beauty, sweet and gift, were presented simultaneously with one group of male names (e.g. Jack, Tom, Bill). More negative words such as bitter, ugly and sad were presented with a different set of male names. The first condition resulted in a positive attitude towards the male names, the second condition in a decrease in positive attitude. Ryan's (1979) research suggested that when children of bilingual parents observe the contexts that accompany use of their second language, such children form negative and positive attitudes towards that language. If the child perceives the contexts as having pleasant enjoyable properties, favourable attitudes may develop towards that second language. For instance, parents taking their children to an enjoyable Welsh-speaking chapel are conditioning attitudes to Welsh by association of speaking Welsh with a pleasurable context. One reason among many why a positive attitude to Welsh declines with age may be due to children perceiving that certain Welsh speaking contexts are not pleasurable, or that English speaking contexts are more pleasurable. Discos, football, popular music and videos provided potentially pleasurable contexts for adolescents which are often English rather than Welsh in language. Such contexts may condition attitudes to second or minority languages.

Reinforcement and operant conditioning

Attitudes may be made more favourable by the suitable arrangement of reward. This is the essence of operant conditioning. Insko (1965) found that students who were reinforced with 'good' when they agreed or disagreed with certain statements of attitude, changed their attitudes over a one week period in the expected direction. Thus maintaining favourable attitudes to minority languages or changing attitudes in a favourable direction may require constant reinforcement. Such reinforcement cannot be arranged in the precisely pre-determined manner of operant conditioning experiments. Nevertheless, institutional and individual reinforcement may be required for favourable language attitudes to be fostered. Children soon learn the positive and negative rewards, outcomes and reinforcements attached to speaking a minority language. Such reinforcements may be non-verbal (e.g. raised eyebrows, smiles) or verbal (e.g. praise, criticism), overt (e.g. congratulated on speaking a second language) or covert (less eye contact from other members in a peer group), individually presented (e.g. reinforcement from a teacher) or expressed publicly (e.g. attributions about Welsh speakers conveyed in the mass media).

Favourable attitudes may be fostered by the experience of success. Perceived success may be critical in establishing positive attitudes. Success of a learner to communicate in an accepted way in a minority language, failure in eisteddfodau competitions, positive or negative experiences in attempted attachment to minority language groups may each affect attitudes.

The reinforcement of attitudes need not be social and external. Self-reinforcement is an important idea especially, but not exclusively in analysing resistance to change. Children's self-control over their aggression is an example of how early parental reinforcement of self control eventually becomes self-reinforcing. Most children achieve self control without the need for external reinforcement. In the same way, attitudes can change from external reinforcement to self reinforcement. Encouragement for a favourable attitude to Irish or Gaelic given early on may eventually become self-reinforcing, partly because such an attitude relates to ego identity, self esteem and self respect. Self reinforcement is also an important concept in that it reveals that external reinforcement may have little or no effect on changing attitudes. Encouragement of a favourable attitude to Welsh may be not enough given self-reinforcement for holding a neutral or unfavourable attitude.

Human modelling

Imitation of someone else may be a powerful source of attitude change. Human models need to be highly regarded, respected, admired and credible in what they say and do. Imitating the attitudes of the model becomes positively reinforcing. The imitator attempts to take on some of the attributes of the favoured model, thus positively affecting feelings of status and worth. Models can range from parents, siblings, peers, teachers, to cultural and media figures.

Attitude may change as a result of the content of a model's speech, conversation or message. Unfortunately, research has failed to give consistent results mainly due to the variety of variables involved and their interactive nature (Kahle, 1984; Cacioppo & Petty, 1982). Who is speaking may be more crucial. Triandis (1971) suggested that physical attractiveness, clothes and speech, expertise, age, race, nationality are some of the variables affecting the persuasiveness of the communicator. Models have to be perceived as having the appropriate status for their verbal communications to effect attitude change. Where the ingroup is a majority language group and the outgroup a minority language group, finding a model to maintain favourable minority language attitude may be difficult.

Consistency and self justification

A variety of social-psychological theories (e.g. Heider, 1958; McGuire, 1981; Festinger, 1957) suggest that attitudes change when an individual has to strive to achieve consistency and an internal logic in attitude systems. For example, it would be difficult for a person to hold a positive attitude to the Welsh language and a negative attitude about bilingual education in Wales. Festinger's (1957) Cognitive Dissonance Theory assumes that our attitudes must be in harmony, but when discordant or cacophonous attitudes arrive, attempts will be made to harmonise and seek concert. When inconsistent attitudes are held, tension may result. There may follow a need to reduce tension by changing one of the attitudes. Cognitive discomfort may require attitude change or attitude rationalisation, especially when the integrity of the self concept is at stake.

A classical piece of research in support of cognitive dissonance theory is by Festinger & Carlsmith (1959). They asked some college students to engage in very boring tasks (e.g. turning a screw through 45 degrees). The monotonous and repetitive tasks lasted an hour. The students were then asked to lie about the task. The students were requested to tell those waiting to perform the same tasks that they were enjoyable, fun, interesting, intriguing and exciting. Some of the students were offered twenty dollars for lying, others were offered just one dollar. A person may be more easily persuaded to act contary to belief if the reward is high. That is, being given twenty dollars (in the mid 1950s) may be seeming justification for lying. A one dollar reward is much less justification, hence there may be more dissonance. To reduce dissonance the subject may decide that the experimental task was fun. The results supported dissonance theory, in that after the experiment, subjects offered one dollar reported that they actually enjoyed the experiment more than did the twenty dollar group.

Operant conditioning theory predicts the opposite: the higher the reward, the more the attitude change. In this situation, striving for consistency seemed to be more important than cash. Cognitive Dissonance theory seems to have strong validity. The theory has received considerable investigation, strong support and refinemen; it has also encountered critiques (e.g. Aronson, 1980; Bem, 1967).

An important piece of research by Bourhis & Giles (1977) shows how cognitive dissonance may work in speech style and identity in Wales. Bourhis & Giles (1977) formed two groups of people from South Wales: those who valued their Welsh identity and those who did not. When engaged in conversation with an English person, the Welsh people who valued their national identity emphasised their less prestigious Welsh accents when the English person derogated Wales. In contrast, Welshmen who did not value their Welsh identity responded to the English person's derogation by attenuating their Welsh accents. In each case, the two groups appeared to obtain cognitive consistency by changing their speech style. The first group did this by becoming more Welsh, thus maintaining harmony with their value of being Welsh. The second group achieved consistency by becoming less Welsh, identifying more with the English speaker and thus harmonising with their lesser valuation of being Welsh.

Attitude change may be induced when discrepant components exist in an attitude. Attitude to a minority language may be positively engendered by the neighbourhood, negatively affected by Anglo pop culture or English language mass media. An individual, in striving for inner consistency, may have to reject one in favour of another. Welsh chapel is spurned; English pop music and discos replace religion. A school where there are cliques of pupils with different language attitudes (e.g. anti-Welsh and anti-English), may require a bilingual and bicultural pupil to develop a partisan attitude. Alternatively, reminding people of their indigenous cultural and language heritage may induce the inconsistency in attitudes which in turn spawns change favourable to an indigenous language.

Language attitudes vary. A few people may have constantly changeable views. Others may hold deep seated convictions that are relatively impervious to persuasion. Where deep seated convictions about a language exist, there is likely to be a strong emotional commitment. Abelson (1988) argued that conviction consists of three factors: emotional commitment, ego preoccupation and cognitive elaboration. Abelson's (1988) studies suggested that convictions may be acquired by learning and thinking first followed by emotional commitment. Alternatively, emotional commitment may precede cognitive deliberation. When emotion (e.g. sudden conversion) comes first, cognitive processes may be distorted in the service of prejudged conclusions (Abelson, 1988). This suggests the narrow line between commitment and fanticism.

Conclusion

Attitude changes both as a function of individual needs and motives and as a function of social situations. The need for success, reward and cognitive consistency interacts with the effect of pleasurable contexts and environments and valued models. Attitudes can change through activity which is self-directed and purposefully planned, as well as through the need for security and status within a group and through societal demands.

Attitude change is essentially a cognitive activity yet is formulated through social activity.

Complementary to examining the relevance of theories of attitude change is an examination of the three overlapping 'who, what and how' issues. Who is likely to effect language attitude change? Parents? Peer groups? Mass media? What situations are associated with attitude change? Teaching? Discussion? Conformity situations? How does change occur? Are there steps in attitude change? The analysis of this chapter adopts part of McGuire's (1985) structure in his review of attitude formation. Details of foundational research on components of this structure may be also found in McGuire (1985). The focus of this chapter is on the implications and message for language attitude change.

Age Changes

As has been discussed in previous chapters, attitudes to language tends to change with age. During the teenage period, attitude to Celtic minority languages tend, as a generalisation, to become less favourable. Research is needed on changes that may occur at different periods (e.g. in the 20s, around the 40s, as older age is reached). Life-span research suggests that some men undergo a midlife crisis around 40 years of age (Levinson, 1978). Around the 40s, a person's life history may be reviewed, past values be re-evaluated, and the future be re-assessed. The age change issue with respect to language attitudes has received little attention. However, it raises the question whether attitude change is purely social or partly physiological. The assumption in social psychology has tended to be that attitude change is through social interaction and environmental experience. Genetic endowment, physiological states, body chemistry and maturation may possibly play a small part in language attitude change. However, age linked changes are more likely to result from social than physiological changes.

Dramatic Experiences

Another implicit assumption in attitude change is often that such changes occur slowly and gradually. They evolve and develop rather than change dramatically and quickly. As McQuire (1985) argues, 'the possibility of sudden ideological shifts deserves sympathetic consideration to counterbalance the strong gradualist bias of twentieth-century science (p. 254). That there can be revolutionary rather than gradual change is witnessed in religious conversion (e.g. John Newton—the hymn writer). Mass attitude shifts were said to have occurred following the assassination of the Civil Rights leader, Martin Luther King (Riley & Pettigrew, 1976).

Language activists sometimes produce situations which potentially cause language attitude shift. Quebec, Israel, the Basque country and Wales have each witnessed well publicised tension and strife. While the clashes may be of a wide political nature in which language is just one element, confrontations may have affected language attitudes. A maiming or killing, personal or non-personal violence, mass protest or guerrilla activity by whatever group may change attitudes 'overnight'. Some may react with hostility to the minority language, others converted to its cause. The publicity of a single significant event may change language attitudes in different directions for different people. Whether the significant event is enacted or imposed by government (e.g. a policy switch) or effected by a group in radical opposition (e.g. setting fire to 'English' owned second homes in Wales), attitudes may quickly change in an intended or unintended manner.

Community Effects

In most minority language communities, there is an uneven balance of minority language speakers and non-speakers. The crucial issue is often who is influencing who? Where, for example, there are English speaking monolingual in-migrants to a Welsh speaking 'heartland' area, does the language attitude of the in-migrants change or the indigenous bilinguals? (Jones, 1990).

Research on racial integration (e.g. Tajfel, 1981) provides some clues about the circumstances that may effect language attitude change when community relationships are considered.

(i) Change may occur when community integration is sustained. Migrant workers who move from job to job, community to community, may be much less likely to change their attitudes to an indigenous language than those who settle in that community. As T.P. Jones (1990) has shown, the rapid turn-over of in-migrants into Welsh heartland communities, provides serious problems for language planning and provision. A fast turn-around in a community also implicates change in attitudes to language in such communities, where polarisation of attitudes may become an instant safeguard.

(ii) Change may occur when it is felt to be voluntary. Imposing conformity in an authoritarian, rule-bound manner is unlikely to change attitude. Informing and consulting, and giving freedom of choice, are paths more likely to lead to language attitude change. Convictions, unlike imposed conformity do not occur instantaneously.

(iii) Change may occur when areas of similarity between monolinguals and bilinguals are used to promote contact. Music, sport, a common goal, religion, hobbies and interests may promote contact, integration and change of attitude. For a minority language speaker, the danger is that common goals and interests will evoke attitude change that is less favourable to that language. Working through a common denominator language (English) may make minority language attitudes less favourable. However, as recent community movements in Ireland and North Wales have shown, when indigenous language groups actively plan contact and events with in-migrants and monolingual individuals, such contact can be on 'minority language terms'.

(iv) Change may occur when relationships between monolingual and bilingual individuals in the community are close, warm, friendly and intimate. Passing sociability does not provide the mechanisms and motivation for attitude change. A bunker attitude to monolinguals by minority language bilinguals often appears to monolinguals as a logical defence of a prized possession. As a Welsh poet, R.S. Thomas, has articulated, being welcoming to the in-migrant English speaking monolingual may be the path to language death. Bunkers can be secure; they are, in the long term, unlikely to succeed. The global village of the twentieth century ensures no long term future for highly protected and introspective minority language communities. A marketing of the minority language seems a more likely route to language maintenance and restoration. Such a marketing would seem to suggest friendship and not separatism as a channel of language attitude change.

(v) Change may occur when the social, economic, political and cultural environment is supportive of minority languages and bilingualism. Communities cannot create attitude change without the conditions for integration and intimacy to occur. Disparity in status or salary between a monolingual and a minority language bilingual, especially when in favour of the former, is tantamount to undermining community integration and consequent language attitude change. Thus in Gwynedd, a county in North Wales, most jobs require fluency in Welsh and English. To be a teacher, administrator, clerk or secretary, the ability to communicate in Welsh and English is often made an essential condition of employment. Recent British educational developments, particularly the formulation of a National Curriculum, have given the Welsh language a more prominent and established place in almost all schools in Wales. Such a supportive ethos of the indigenous language at a government level is an important foundation for community efforts in language attitude change.

Parental Effects

The influence of parental language attitudes on children's language attitudes is likely to be considerable. In previous chapters, where language background was entered into attitude equations, the implicit belief was that the language of the home has an impact on attitudes. The moderate correlations between language background and attitude have confirmed this. There is a danger, however. That children's attitudes tend to match, or be similar, to their parents, does not imply that one causes the other. A high correspondence may be due to effects of relations, neighbours, friends and school. Cross-generational similarities in terms of community, economic conditions, and especially cultural experiences may underlie parental effects rather than, or as well as, parental indoctrination.

Some children grow up with opposite views to their parents. Such a reaction to parents could indeed demonstrate the effect of parental influence. Parents who are strongly anti-minority language may provoke a pro-minority language reaction in their offspring. However, the more customary situation seems to be congruence between parental and child language attitudes, with mechanisms such as introjection, modelling, identification, rewards and punishments and social comparison, contributing to that congruence.

Peer Group Effects

It is popular to believe that familial influence on language attitudes has weakened this century, with other socialisation agencies such as peer groups and mass media having increasing effects. As has been argued in previous chapters, youth culture appears to have a relatively strong effect on language attitudes. Involvement in 'pop' culture may be related to groups of children becoming more Anglicised, and less favourable in attitude to the Welsh language. Also, involvement in Welsh cultural agencies (e.g. Yr Urdd (Welsh League of Youth), Eisteddfodau, Church or Chapel) may result in the preservation of a more favourable attitude to Welsh. McGuire (1985) summarises such peer group influence:

> Urbanisation, population growth, and mass media technology that bring large numbers of homogeneously aged children into contact or expose them to common experiences have produced a distinctive centripetal youth culture as regards art forms, values, and life styles (p. 255).

Institutional Effects

Various institutions may affect language attitudes. Through the status given to a language (e.g. the use of Welsh in law courts, banks, civil service, local government, shops) and through the teaching of a language (e.g. in school, adult classes) attitudes to a language may change. A language that has no place in daily business, administration and transactions, is likely to be linked with attitude 'decline'. When a minority language is the modus operandi in public transactions and discourse, attitudes may stay or become more favourable. In Wales, strong and successful attempts have been made for Welsh to become increasingly part of institutional life. Receiving communications in Welsh and English, being able to speak Welsh to the bank cashier and write cheques in Welsh, giving evidence in Welsh in courts, bilingual road signs, some government documents being bilingual and a Welsh TV channel all join to create an environment where Welsh may be perceived as having utilitarian value and functional vitality. Rather than Welsh being relegated to the chapel and eisteddfod field, Welsh has blossomed at an institutional level. Increasing the prestige of a language by institutional activity in that language, provides the conditions for the evolution of more favourable attitudes.

Of all the institutions that may be linked with attitude change, school is often regarded as the most influential. Attending a bilingual or monolingual school, delivery of the curriculum in a minority language, using that minority language in extra-curricular activities and in the hidden curriculum are all expected to change language attitudes. By the language used to communicate the curriculum, by cultural lessons (e.g. History, Geography, Social and Personal Development), via the language of playground and sports field, language attitudes may evolve and change. The recent studies on school effectiveness have demonstrated that similar pupils are affected differently by differing schools (Rutter et al., 1979; Smith & Tomlinson, 1989; Mortimore et al., 1988; Reynolds, 1985).

Mass Media Effects

Popular belief asserts that mass media affects attitudes in an influential manner. Overall, research suggests that mass media does not have large effects on public attitudes (McGuire, 1985). Television, records, cassettes, videos, satellite broadcasts, films, radio and computer software are often regarded as having an influence on the language attitudes of teenagers in particular. The research of E.P. Jones (1982), further analysed in Baker (1985), suggested that mass media effects on language attitudes were small, unexpectedly so. More active, participatory cultural forms (e.g. eisteddfodau) were found to be more influential in changing language attitudes between the ages of 10 and 13. As the research in this book has indicated, mass media are only one part of teenage culture. A study by Baker & Waddon (1990) suggested that youth culture is essentially about values, mores, customs and conventions. Mass media are only one input into conventions and intentions. Despite the long hours of viewing of television, despite its presentation of social values, the suggestion of research is that we too easily over-emphasise the effect of mass media. Being such an obvious and ever-present article of daily life may lead to the exaggeration of the actual influence of mass media on language attitudes. Nevertheless, some influence must be assumed.

Rituals

Attitudes may be changed by a variety of ritual and ceremonial devices aimed at influencing language use and attitude. A May Day parade or pageantry may be partly to influence attitudes to a nation. In Wales, the eisteddfodic rituals, with chaired Bards, the orders of green, blue and white druids, the ceremony to crown the winning poets, the ritual hymn singing at Cardiff Arms Park before international rugby matches may each and all stimulate favourable attitudes to Welsh.

Situational Effects

The discussion of question 'who effects language attitude change?' has beneath it the question of 'what situations engender attitude change?' McGuire (1985) lists five types of situation.

(i) *Mass media*. Mass media provide a one direction flow of information. A person is passive, unable to participate by presenting alternative attitudes. Putting a person into a non-active, receive-only mode may account for mass media not being the most influential source of language attitude change.

(ii) *Suggestion*. A suggestion situation is where repetitive provision of information is made. No arguments for a change of attitude are presented. In Wales, language activists sometimes write slogans on walls and in public places. 'Addysg Gymraeg' (a call for Welsh medium education) and 'Cymraeg—iaith ein plant?' (a call to preserve Welsh in the language of children) are two examples. Attitude change towards Welsh is hoped for by the suggestibility of slogans. Persuasion is attempted by punchy public phrases. The millions of pounds spent on advertisements on undergrounds and billboards attests to the belief that brevity has benefits.

(iii) *Group Discussion*. Group discussion is different from mass media and repetitive suggestions due to the intended active participation of the group members. Individual attitudes may be expressed, explored, and may evolve. Discussion, for example, of the uses and value of a minority language may reveal not only agreements and disagreements, but alternative ideas not previously considered or ideas that are more complex and multidimensional than first conceived. Such discussions need not be formal—as in discussions in the street, in the tavern or at a meal.

(iv) *Conformity.* Some situations may seek to induce attitude change by attempting conformity. Being made to feel 'the odd person out', as when language causes individual ostracism in a group. The in-migrant, for example, may be pressured by a group to attend language classes. Acceptance is the promised prise, although not always delivered. Exclusion from social acceptance is the punishment for failing to conform. Conformity in minority language communities may depend on the balance of power, saturation of speakers and perceived cost-benefit balance of conformity.

(v) *Indoctrination.* When great control is made of stimuli, response possibilities, motivational states and reinforcements, indoctrination may occur. While such changes tend to be associated with political prisoners, religious 'cult' communities, extreme youth political movements and some military operations, some of the routes to indoctrination are worth listing:
 • depersonalisation
 • weakening confidence
 • confusing with discrepant information
 • monopolising communication
 • instigating guilt and shame, increasing anxiety

The list provides a suggestion of what needs to be avoided in changing attitudes in a democratic society.

Summary and Conclusion

This chapter has attempted to focus on the major influences of language attitude change. As well as looking at attitude change theories as applicable to language attitudes and the elements of persuasive communication, language attitude change has been viewed in terms of institutional systems. It was suggested that language attitude change gathers important insights from an historical perspective. Language attitudes evolve over decades, and social historians have a vital role in analysing the reasons for such historical changes.

A systems approach to language change will highlight institutions that affect change. This chapter has spotlighted parents, community, peer groups, schools and mass media as examples of influencers of attitude change. Such institutions provide a variability of influence, ranging from simple suggestibility to indoctrination.

One important conclusion is reached. While attitude change has been a well researched topic in social psychology since the 1960s, there is a dire need to study attitude change with regard to languages. Why do some indigenous minority language speakers develop less favourable, even unfavourable attitudes to that language? Why do some majority language speakers wish to learn a minority language and develop a positive attitude to that language and culture?

Language ecology requires explanations of attitude shift. Language death, restoration, preservation or resurrection can be assumed to have strong links with language attitudes. While linguists (e.g. Dorian, 1981) and sociolinguists (e.g. Fishman, 1976, 1990) have made an input into the explanation of language shift, social psychology has been notably reluctant to address this important issue, despite a wealth of theory and research on attitude change. This chapter has attempted some connections between attitude as discussed in social psychology and language shift. The next chapter attempts some research.

6 Language and Attitude Change: A Research Perspective

Introduction and Aims

The aim of this chapter is to investigate the change in attitudes that took place in the research sample over two years. The aim of the second testing was not to explore whether any one theory of attitude change was more or less valid. That is, the aims were not to test psychological theory. Rather the issues spotlighted were derived from previous Welsh research and from issues located in previous chapters and are as follows:

- Did attitudes become more or less favourable over the two years?

The children were initially tested at age 11 to 14 when in the first, second and third year of Secondary education. At the second testing, the ages spanned from 13 to 16. The first year had become third years, the second years had become fourth years in their Secondary schools. The third year had become fifth years—the earliest point at which such pupils can leave school and enter work. The general question is whether language attitudes become more or less favourable over the two years.

- Which particular groups of children change the most over two years?

Such a question can be addressed by comparing girls and boys, those from different language backgrounds, different age groups, varying ability levels, the three different schools and different patterns of youth culture. The expected change was towards attitudes becoming less favourable. In terms of language maintenance, it is also valuable to highlight those whose attitudes stay, or become, relatively favourable. Therefore, the third issue addressed became:

- What are the characteristics of those whose language attitudes tend to stay, or become relatively favourable?

In order to locate different types of children, a cluster analysis was performed. This analyses all the children and all the relevant variables in one overall investigation. Groups of similar children are located and portrayed. The chapter then integrates the variables into overall LISREL models of language change. The logic of this is to find major and minor effects on language attitude change. Thus the fourth question posed is:

• Which variables are more and less influential in language attitude change?

Background

Sample

The second testing followed a time span of two years after the first testing. During that time, some children had left the three schools. Others had joined the schools after the first testing. The total number of completed questionnaires from the second testing was 798. One hundred and forty one of these were 'new' since the first testing (17.7%). The spread in change of pupils between testings was relatively even across the three schools.

The inward and outward movement of pupils between the testings would not seem to affect the analysis on the overall sample. There is no evidence in the data that the incomers were different in any major way to the outgoers. However, when analyses (presented later) concern the reduced sample, some bias in sample may exist. The reduced sample comprises those for whom there are data from both testings. This longitudinal sample does not contain pupils whose families are more itinerant. Families who are socially and vocationally mobile as well as geographically mobile tend to give the reduced sample a small bias. Thus the 'change' results on the reduced sample probably apply to the more static and rooted groups. This limits the generalisation of the results, and creates a need for replication studies.

Variables

Data on the same variables as in the first testing were collected: language background, self-perceived ability in Welsh, youth culture, attitudes to Welsh and bilingualism. To test whether the *structure* of attitudes and language background changed over time, the same scale items were used as in the first testing. That is, items on the attitude and youth culture scales which received low latent variable loadings were included in the second questionnaire. Such scales could then be examined for change in structure and content when used with older age groups.

The language background of individuals changed little over time (r = 0.84) and investigations revealed no substance in the minor changes. Ability in Welsh gave a similar quasi-normal distribution as in the first testing. The Youth Culture questionnaire was latent variable analysed, as before, and gave the same two latent variables (Welsh and Literary Culture and 'Popular' Culture). The loadings of items on the two latent variables was highly comparable to the first testing and are therefore not presented.

Latent variable analysis of the attitude scales revealed two replications of the first testing, and one major difference. The attitude to bilingualism scale and the general attitude to Welsh scale both clearly fitted one latent variable. Item loadings were very similar to the first testing. Attitude to the uses and value of Welsh changed between testings. It was expected the same two latent variables would re-appear, namely instrumental and integrative attitudes to Welsh. The eigenvalues of the latent variable analysis in the second testing indicated the presence of one rather than two latent variables. When two latent variables were rotated, the solution did not represent a clear instrumental/integrative divide. On the second testing, the 'uses and functions of Welsh' scale was reduced to one latent variable.

The suggestion is, therefore, that language attitude structure may change with age. It might be expected that, as age increases, cognitions about language attitude become more differentiated and complex. The unexpected finding here is that with increasing age, attitude to language becomes more unified and centred. The question becomes 'at what age does the change in structure tend to occur?' To answer this, a separate latent variable analysis was run for the differing age group from both the first and second testings. The results suggested that it is during the third year of secondary education (13–14 years old) the structural change occurs. When the teenage years commence, language attitudes appear to change towards being less favourable to Welsh and more unidimensional.

A further single latent variable analysis was performed on the three attitude scales: attitude to bilingualism, use of Welsh and general attitude to Welsh. This is important in testing the stability of the latent variable solutions found in the first testing, where the three scales were independently isolated by the latent variable analysis. An overall latent variable analysis also tests whether the use of older age groups produces a different solution to that found with younger age groups.

A latent variable analysis of the 65 items indicated the presence of three latent variables. Latent variable two reproduced the Uses of Welsh scale, with all 20 items loading above 0.45 on that latent variable. Latent variable three reproduced the attitude to bilingualism items. However, seven of the

25 attitude to bilingualism items did not load above 0.30 on latent variable three. Latent variable one was slightly less clear-cut than in the first testing. The general attitude to Welsh scale provided the high loadings on that latent variable, with 17 out of 20 items with values above 0.30. At the same time, two 'use of Welsh' and 11 'attitude to bilingualism' items had substantial (0.30 and over) loadings on that latent variable. This suggests that general attitude to bilingualism is closer to general attitude to Welsh than general attitude to Welsh is to uses of Welsh.

Reliabilities

As in the first testing, the reliabilities (Cronbach's alpha) of the various latent variable scales were computed. This is particularly for later insertion in LISREL models. The coefficients were as follows:

Youth Culture (Welsh & Literacy)	= 0.69
Youth Culture (Popular)	= 0.67
Language Background	= 0.98
Uses of Welsh (Attitude)	= 0.95
General Attitude to Welsh	= 0.92
Attitude to Bilingualism	=0.92

The reliability coefficients indicate high internal consistency on the attitude scales and language background scale. The measures of internal reliability of the two youth culture scales are not so high. Coefficients above 0.80 are generally sought; these two youth culture scales fall to 0.7.

The size of the reliability coefficients can affect the solution of a LISREL model. Lower reliabilities sometimes boost the size of the path coefficients from scales with lower reliabilities (Cuttance & Ecob, 1988). Therefore simulation of the models with higher youth culture reliabilities were run. The final models presented appear robust enough with simulated changes in youth culture reliabilities. The tendency is that the final models slightly under emphasise language background. Such simulations did not suggest distortion in the result but the need for care in using lower reliabilities. Having dealt with background analyses, the four issues will now be addressed.

Issue One : Did Attitudes Become More or Less Favourable Over the Two Years?

To tackle the question posed, the changes over two years in the three scales will be detailed. This initial question is rather bland, in that it does not examine precisely who changes. This is examined later. The initial analysis is of the sample as a whole.

The analysis focuses on individual items and not on latent variable scores. Latent variable scores from the first and second testing have a 'forced' mean of zero (50 when changed to 'T' scores). Therefore it is inappropriate to use latent variable scores to indicate change. Instead, the list below indicates the quantity of individual attitude items that changed.

Attitude to the uses of Welsh

Over the 20 items on the Attitude to the Uses of Welsh scale, there was a statistically significant (< 0.05) movement on 19 items. All 19 items showed the same direction of movement, regarding the Welsh language as less important. This suggests that as children become older, their perception changes to Welsh being less important. On both instrumental and integrative items, attitude to Welsh became less favourable. The only item where there was no statistically significant change was 'Watching TV/Videos'. On none of the items was the change as large as one category (e.g. 'important' to 'a little important'). Thus the change is definite but small.

General attitude to the Welsh language

The general attitude to Welsh scale contained 20 items. On half of the items a statistically significant change was located. These 10 statements are listed below.

I prefer to watch TV in English than Welsh.
I like speaking Welsh.
Welsh is a difficult language to learn.
There are more useful languages to learn than Welsh.
Welsh is a language worth learning.
Welsh is essential to take part fully in Welsh life.
Children should not be made to learn Welsh.
It's hard to study Science in Welsh.
You are considered a lower class person if you speak Welsh.
I prefer to be taught in Welsh.

On nine of the ten items listed above, the direction of change was the same. Attitudes to Welsh became less favourable. Thus reactions to positive items (e.g. 'I like speaking Welsh') tended to be less positive than two years before. Reaction to negatively worded items (e.g. 'Welsh is a difficult language to learn') also indicated less favourability than before. The changes were not large, mostly less than a category.

The odd item from the ten was 'You are considered a lower class person if you speak Welsh'. As children become older, they tended to disagree more with this statement. Whether this indicates a growth in favourability or unfavourability will vary from person to person. A value judgment is required about what is 'favourable' or not. The change may indicate less willingness to stereotype or pigeon-hole as teenagers become older.

Attitude to bilingualism

On this 25 item scale, 12 items showed change over the two years. As with the general attitude scale, this indicates (as does the small size of the changes) that change is definite but not great.

Where there is change, it is mostly towards attitudes to bilingualism becoming less favourable. Of the 12 items where there was a statistically significant movement over the two years, ten changed towards less favourability. These ten items are:

To speak one language in Wales is all that is needed.
Knowing Welsh and English makes people cleverer.
Being able to write in English and Welsh is important.
All schools in Wales should teach pupils to speak in Welsh and English.
Knowing both Welsh and English gives people problems.
I feel sorry for people who cannot speak both English and Welsh.
People know more if they speak English and Welsh.
People who speak Welsh and English can have more friends than those who speak one language.
Speaking both Welsh and English help people get promotion in their job.
People only need to know one language.

As with the two previously considered attitude scales, it is wrong to conclude that attitudes become unfavourable. The movement tends to be from being more to less favourable and from being mostly favourable to being neutral. There is thus an important distinction between the amount of change and the direction of that change. The ten items listed above indicate areas of significant change (amount). This is separate from 'where to where' the change has occurred (direction).

Two items became more favourable to bilingualism over time:

Young children learn to speak Welsh and English at the same time with ease.
I should not like English to take over from the Welsh.

This indicates that age changes are not always in one direction. As cognitions about language change, so may attitudes to specific issues. Early childhood bilingualism and English language supremacy both seem to be areas where increasing age leads to more pro-bilingualism views.

Having discovered that, where attitude change exists, it is predominantly towards decreased favourability, the chapter refines the analysis to locate more precisely where change is occurring.

Issue Two: Which Particular Groups of Children Change the Most Over Two Years?

So far, consideration of change in attitudes over the two years has looked at general, average change. This expresses information about everybody and nobody at the same time. Some children may have changed considerably, others hardly at all. Some may have changed positively; some may have stayed the same; a greater number are likely to have changed negatively. Do girls change more than boys? At what age is there the most change? How does school, ability in Welsh, youth culture and language background relate to change in attitudes?

Before examining these questions individually and then as a whole, a point about attitude change needs to be made. Change in attitude should not be measured by the difference between initial and final scores on each of the items nor on latent variables. A pupil who already has a favourable attitude has little room to show increased favourability. Someone with a neutral or unfavourable initial attitude has relatively greater room to show improvement. Thus residualised change scores were used rather than simple change scores (Youngman, 1979). A residualised change score is the difference between an expected or predicted final score and the actual final score. With residual change scores, a zero score implies no change. Such change scores were calculated for the three attitude scales and the two youth culture scales by using the latent variable scores. This entailed reducing the uses of Welsh attitude scale to one dimension on both testings. Such scores could only be calculated for those with data from both testings (maximum $N = 656$).

Gender

On the two attitude to Welsh scales, males became less favourable to Welsh than did females over the two year period. Decline in positive attitude was more evident among males than females ($p < 0.05$) on the Uses of Welsh and general Attitude to Welsh scales. No statistically significant gender differences were found on changes in attitude to bilingualism.

Age

No statistically significant differences were found in change of attitude between different age groups. The movement over the two year time lap was similar for the different age groups. The move towards less favourable attitudes on all three attitude scales was comparable for the 12 to 14 year olds as the 14 to 16 years olds. Given that the steepest gradient of descent in favourable attitudes was found between 13 and 14 year olds in the first, cross-sectional testing (see Chapter 3), the expectation was that most change might be located among those who were 13 at the first testing and 14 and 15 at the second testing. However, decline in the longitudinal analysis appears to be approximately the same for the different age groups. It should not be forgotten that the structural change occurs at around 14 years of age.

School

On all three attitude scales, one school showed a much higher change rate than the others ($p < 0.00001$). The English medium school was connected with the greatest decrease in positive attitudes. No statistically significant difference was found between the natural Welsh and the designated bilingual school. Change in attitude to Welsh and change in attitude to bilingualism is particularly located within an Anglicised community, as is illustrated in Figure 6.1.

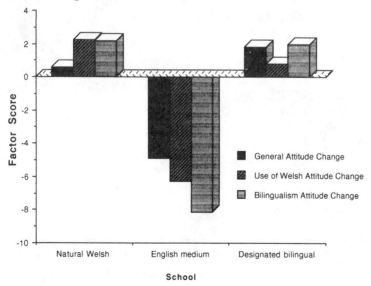

Figure 6.1

One cannot conclude that it is the school which is the causal factor in itself. Is the causal effect on attitude change in the home, the community, due to youth culture as well as, or instead of the school? This issue is considered when constructing the LISREL models (presented later).

Language background

The effect of out of school influences on attitude change may be partly estimated by language background. On all three attitude scales, language background correlated with language attitude change. The correlations for the use of Welsh, general attitude to Welsh and attitude to bilingualism scales were respectively 0.09, 0.09 and 0.18. The correlations, although statistically significant are small. In comparison, the correlation between school (Welsh compared with English medium) and attitude change was respectively 0.32, 0.24 and 0.16. This hints that school may be a larger influence than language background.

There is a second way the relationship between language background and attitude change can be examined. Comparisons of attitude change across the four language clusters provides a typification of who changes.

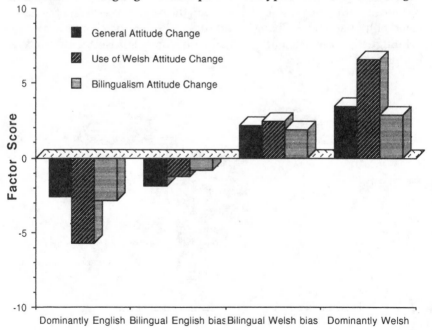

Figure 6.2

On all three attitude scales, the same (statistically) significant rank ordering of the four language clusters was found. The order from most to least change is as follows:

Most change   1. Dominantly English language background

                          2. Bilingual, bias towards English background

                          3. Bilingual, bias toward Welsh background

Least change   4. Dominantly Welsh language background

This is illustrated and expanded in Figure 6.2.

Those who become less favourable in their attitudes over the two years are those from the more English language backgrounds. The more Welsh the language background, the higher the probability of less change and staying favourable in language attitudes.

Ability in Welsh

Pupils with higher (self perceived) ability in Welsh tended to retain more favourable language attitudes on all three latent attitude variables. Those with lower self-reported Welsh language ability tended to become less favourable in their language attitudes. The correlations between attitude change and perceived ability are presented below:

Change in

      1. Attitude to the Use of Welsh $r = 0.17$

      2. General Attitude to Welsh $r = 0.21$

      3. Attitude to Bilingualism $r = 0.30$

Youth Culture

A change in language attitude is linked with an increasing use of 'popular' culture (e.g. discos, same sex and opposite sex friendships). The correlations here range between 0.08 and 0.10. Larger correlations are found between a decreasing involvement in Welsh and literary youth culture (e.g. attending eisteddfodau, going to a Welsh chapel, using the library) and a decline in attitude to the Welsh language.

Correlations between a decrease in participation in Welsh and literary culture and language attitude change are relatively substantial, as follows:

Change in

         1. Attitude to the Use of Welsh $r = 0.32$

         2. General Attitude to Welsh $r = 0.31$

        3. Attitude to Bilingualism $r = 0.29$

Thus change in youth culture and the school attended appear, on first analyses, to be the factors most associated with attitude change. Further analyses (2 and 3 way ANOVAs) were run to detect any interaction between age, gender, school and language clusters. No statistically significant interactions were found.

This section has indicated which groups of children appear to have declined in attitude to Welsh. There are two dangers. First, it may be naive to believe that school and youth culture are the important factors. While this seems so from the results of this section, a model of attitude change (presented later) estimates the extent of these effects and considers inter-relationship between these factors. Thus, what appears the effect of schooling, may be better attributed to another factor or factors correlated with schooling. Second, there is an ideological danger of only examining 'downward' decline in minority language attitudes. It is too often the case that research examines the correlates of decreasing favourability in language attitude. While this may be the major or overall pattern, there will be those whose attitudes stay favourable, even become favourable. Thus, a balanced approach may usefully focus on both decline and maintenance. Therefore, the third question examined becomes:

Issue Three: What are the Characteristics of Those Whose Language Attitudes Tend to Stay or Become Relatively Favourable?

To determine the characteristics of those whose language attitude do not decline, there are two methods of approach. First, it seems possible to extract those scores which do not change over the two years, or even become more favourable. There are major problems with this. Both latent variable scores and residualised gain scores do not indicate unambiguously who has demonstrated language maintenance or positive change. Latent variable scores and residualised gain scores become standardised, often with a mean of zero and a standard deviation of one. Such standardisation therefore prevents location of those who have stayed favourable or become more favourable in their language attitudes. A positive residualised gain score is a comparison with the average person. It may hide an absolute decline in attitude. Using the raw gain scores on individual items has problems of scaling, dimensionality, item reliability and size of gain possible. Thus simple raw gain scores are also inappropriate.

A favoured approach is the use of cluster analysis. By taking all pupils for whom there is complete data over the two years, cluster analysis produces groups with similar profiles. Such an analysis is preferred as it does not produce an *a priori* 'maintenance' group. That is, there may be two or more profiles of pupils whose attitudes do not become less favourable over time.

The following 13 variables were entered into the cluster analysis:

Gender
Age
School
Language Background (first testing)
Ability in Welsh (first testing)
Ability in Welsh (second testing)
Youth Culture (baseline, first testing)—Welsh and Literary Culture
Youth Culture (baseline, first testing)—Popular Culture
Change in Welsh and Literary Culture (residualised change scores)
Change in Popular Culture (residualised change scores)
Change in Attitude to the Uses of Welsh (residualised change scores)
Change in General Attitude to Welsh (residualised change scores)
Change in Attitude to Bilingualism (residualised change scores)

A three cluster solution best fitted the data. No differences of age were found between the three groups. The profile of the differences between the three groups is provided in Table 6.1.

There are two clusters of minor interest. Cluster one contains approximately half of the sample and is average on most variables. Its one distinguishing feature is a considerable movement away from Welsh and literary culture over the two years. Cluster Three is clearly a group who show the relatively greatest decline in attitude to Welsh and bilingualism. Such a decline appears to co-exist with an English language background and a movement away from Welsh and literary culture.

One cluster is of major interest. Cluster Two, containing one in three of the sample, appears (not unambiguously) to contain those whose language attitudes are maintained over the two year period. On each of the three attitude scales, this group uniformly showed a high positive attitude score relative to the average. Concomitants of language attitude maintenance are a strong Welsh language background, relatively strong involvement in Welsh and literary culture, higher than average ability in Welsh and being in Welsh medium education. There is also relatively less involvement in 'popular' culture, and decreasing involvement in that culture over time.

It remains to examine which of these variables are the most and least influential. The cluster analysis suggest which variables are important, not the degree of that importance.

Table 6.1

	Cluster One	Cluster Two	Cluster Three
% of Sample	44%	33.5%	22.5%
Gender	No Bias	Female Bias	No Bias
School	Welsh Medium bias	Welsh Medium	English Medium bias
Language Background	49.4	60.2	45.1
Ability in Welsh (first testing)	3.2	3.6	3.1
Ability in Welsh (second testing)	2.9	3.7	2.4
Welsh & Literary Culture (baseline)	48.4	57.1	47.1
Popular Culture (baseline)	50.1	47.5	50.2
Change in Welsh & Literary Culture	-2.1	+5.9	-4.7
Change in Popular Culture	+0.2	-1.5	+1.9
Change in Attitude to Use of Welsh	+0.3	+7.1	-11.3
Change in General Attitude to Welsh	-0.3	+8.6	-12.2
Change in Attitude to Bilingualism	+0.4	+7.2	-11.4

Issue Four: Which Variables are More and Less Influential in Language Attitude Change?

A complex longitudinal model was constructed to examine the paths of attitude change. It is summarised in simplified form in Figure 6.3.

The results of testing the change models are now presented. First, attitude to bilingualism is considered followed by the two measures of attitude to Welsh (uses and general attitude). Since the path diagrams are complicated, even without the coefficients, the basic results are presented below, with full details in Appendix 2.

Change in attitude to bilingualism

At the root of the analysis is the relative influence of school, home and youth culture on change in attitude to bilingualism. What most influences

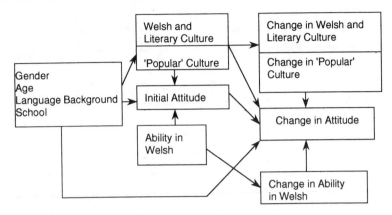

Figure 6.3

language attitude change? The relatively stable language background of the home and community, the youth culture that is adopted or the effect of personal characteristics such as gender?

Following the reduction of the sample from the first to second testing, the correlation between language background and school (Welsh medium compared with English medium) becomes high (0.93). Following 'drop-out' (often children from English language backgrounds in Welsh medium education, but also children from Welsh language backgrounds in English medium education), language background and school become too similar to use as separate entities. For the LISREL analysis to run successfully, school was, of necessity, combined with language background. Thus school is not lost, but is subsumed under the heading of language background, using data on language background as the overall indicator.

For attitude to bilingualism, the major paths (coefficients above 0.35) are represented in Figure 6.4. In the diagram, the absence of ability in Welsh, age and gender indicates that these variables do not figure in any major way in predicting change in attitude to bilingualism. The influence on attitude change comes predominantly from the cultural factors. The language background of the home (and by implication, the school) are not major direct effects on attitude change. Language background is only an indirect influence on the preference for a Welsh and literary culture. The size of these direct and indirect effects is given in Table 6.2.

The LISREL model suggests the influence on attitude change is through both participation in different forms of teenage culture, and through movements during the two year period towards 'popular' youth culture. Indeed participation in youth culture is apparently more powerful than a favourable initial attitude to Welsh. Of the different forms of youth culture,

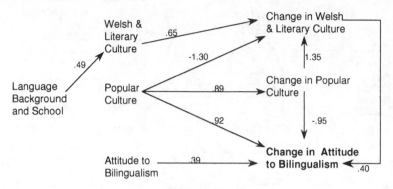

Figure 6.4

the form that seems most to lead to attitude change is popular culture (e.g. discos, same-sex and opposite-sex friendships). The indirect effect of popular culture through its effect on Welsh literary culture appears to lead strongly to attitude change. 'Popular' culture itself has a strong direct effect on attitude change, both in amount of participation and change towards more participation in 'popular' culture in the two years.

A simplified expression of the LISREL analysis is that the language background of home and school affects participation in Welsh cultural forms. Such participation in Welsh cultural forms is markedly influenced by popular culture during the teenage years. The level of interest in popular culture and the increased interest in popular culture over the two years appear high up the list of effects on change in attitude to bilingualism.

Table 6.2 Effects of variables on change in attitude to bilingualism

	Total Effects	Indirect Effects
Gender	0.00	–0.12
Age	0.00	–0.03
Language Background/School	0.37	0.24
Welsh and Literary Culture (initial level)	0.15	0.38
Popular Culture (initial level)	0.02	–0.90
Attitude to Bilingualism (initial level)	0.45	0.06
Ability in Welsh (initial level)	0.05	0.14
Change in Welsh and Literary Culture	–0.33	0.62
Change in Popular Culture	0.41	0.01
Change in Ability in Welsh	0.23	0.00

Change in general attitude to Welsh

A fairly similar patterning occurred for general attitude to Welsh compared with attitude to bilingualism. The number of relatively strong paths tends to be more. The essential skeleton of the final LISREL model is given in Figure 6.5, followed by an effects table (Table 6.3).

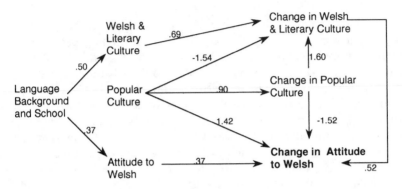

Figure 6.5

Table 6.3 Effects of variables on change in general attitude to Welsh

	Total Effects	Indirect Effects
Gender	0.06	–0.23
Age	0.03	–0.01
Language Background/School	0.50	0.31
Welsh and Literary Culture (initial level)	0.17	0.46
'Popular' Culture (initial level)	–0.02	–0.45
Attitude to Welsh (initial level)	0.39	0.02
Ability in Welsh (initial level)	0.07	0.16
Change in Welsh and Literary Culture	–0.61	0.90
Change in 'Popular/' Culture	0.53	0.01
Change in Ability in Welsh	0.19	0.00

In terms of change in attitude to Welsh over the two years, the strongest direct effects are level of participation in popular culture and increasing use of that form of culture over the two year period. L anguage background (home and school) has an indirect effect rather than direct effect, influencing involvement in Welsh and literary culture and the initial level of attitude to Welsh. Increased exposure to popular culture appears to invoke a change in utilisation of Welsh and literary culture. A decrease in the use of Welsh and literary culture has a direct effect on decreasing favourability of attitudes to Welsh. Of the four major direct effects, 'popular' culture, in its level of involvement and in its change over the two years, is the most influential. Gender, age and ability in Welsh, although included in the model, have small or minimal effects. That is, change in attitude to Welsh occurs across the two gender, across the three different age groups and across different ability levels.

If the model is used to highlight those who do not become less favourable in their attitude to Welsh, the following profile is possible. Such a person is likely to come from a relatively strong Welsh language background (home and school) with an initial positive attitude to Welsh and relatively strong participation in Welsh cultural forms. The less the experience of popular culture at an earlier age the better. Early involvement in popular culture, even with a Welsh language background (home and school) and an initially favourable attitude to Welsh, is likely to be a root cause of change in attitude. Such early involvement in popular culture is likely to lead to a decreased involvement in Welsh and literary culture, increased involvement in popular culture and a decline in favourability of attitude to Welsh.

The model thus suggests the early level of participation in popular culture is the pivot around which future attitude turns.

Change in attitude to the uses of Welsh

The third analysis, concerning change in attitude to the uses and functions of Welsh, is similar to the above analyses. Popular culture is again the central variable around which attitude change occurs. When the world of pop music, discos, groups and gangs occurs early in late childhood, less

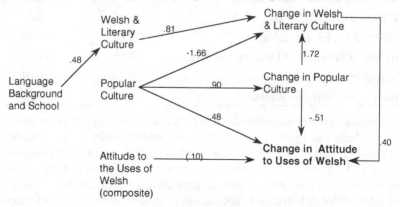

Figure 6.6 The model

favourable attitudes to the use of Welsh tend to result. Such a 'popular' orientation is likely to affect Welsh cultural activity and affect instrumental and integrative attitudes.

Table 6.4 Effects of variables on uses of Welsh

	Total Effects	Indirect Effects
Gender	0.03	–0.02
Age	–0.01	–0.02
Language Background/School	0.39	0.12
Welsh & Literary Culture (initial level)	0.17	0.33
Popular Culture (initial level)	–0.03	–0.50
Attitude to Use of Welsh (initial level)	–0.14	–0.04
Ability in Welsh (initial level)	0.07	0.07
Change in Welsh & Literary Culture	0.24	0.75
Change in Popular Culture	0.41	0.01
Change in Ability in Welsh	0.19	0.00

Summary

This chapter has focused on the correlates of changing attitude over the two years. Simple analyses of which groups change followed by complex analyses by structural equation modelling have tended to produce a consensus.

While boys are slightly more likely to decline in favourability of attitude than girls, change occurs across both genders. While it was expected that older children would decline more in favourability of attitude, this was not the case. However, the third form in secondary school (age 13 and 14) appears the pivotal time when structural change occurs. Yet the analyses do not point to increasing age in itself as a crucial influencing factor. Ability in Welsh also does not come out as very important. Change in attitude occurs across different ability levels.

Language background does appear to have an effect on attitudes, particular when combined with participation in Welsh cultural forms and with the relative absence of 'popular' culture. Language background (combining home, community and school) does not turn out to be the major determinant of change. The pivot seems 'popular' culture. A child who engages in 'popular' culture early is likely to be the one with a higher predictability of attitude decline. A Welsh language background may decrease the probability of a direct link between popular culture and decline in attitude. A Welsh language background is insufficient insurance.

Engaging popular culture tends to affect a child's participation in Welsh and literary cultural activity. Decreased participation in Welsh cultural activity (e.g. eisteddfodau, religious affiliation) leads to less favourable attitudes to Welsh. However, the larger influence, directly and indirectly, is participation in 'popular' culture. Such a lifestyle seems to have the largest effect on declining attitude.

Is there an inevitable paradox? Attitude to Welsh is strongest when children are relatively unfamiliar with popular culture and participate more in traditional Welsh culture and engage more in the less gregarious activity of private reading. The global village, the breakdown in European barriers, the glamour and glitter of Anglo-American culture may make it more and more difficult to adopt an isolationist approach to Welsh culture. Biculturalism becomes the easy slogan. On these analyses, biculturalism can be seen either as a threat or as the challenge to be met in the salvation of the language. Biculturalism may open the door to wide and varied experiences but in walks popular, modern, majority culture. In a teenager's living space such culture may leave decreasing room for a minority language.

Postscript: Perspectives and Prospects

The Prologue indicated that the intention of the book was to address five issues from the theoretical and research literature on attitudes and language. No book will close the gaps in language attitude literature. It can only attempt to fill some of the space and glimpse the areas yet to be covered. This final chapter notes what space may have been filled by this book and then indicates the areas that still need to be addressed.

The first issue was defined as the relationship between general attitude theory and research and language attitudes. Attitude theory has a long and distinguished history and therefore research on language attitudes can usefully engage that history. There are conceptual distinctions and measurement guidelines still valuable: the cognitive, affect and behavioural triad is one example; some of the principles from Likert, Thurstone and Semantic Differential attitude measurement are still relevant. In the same way, recent developments in attitude theory can valuably be taken on board to refine and sophisticate language attitude research.

This translates into an appeal for those who are concerned with language attitudes to root their understanding in the rich soil of general attitude theory and research. Just as the vineyard keeper needs to understand basic agricultural principles as well as having specific knowledge of grape production, so with language attitudes. A fine wine is not produced by guesswork or novice entrepreneurs. The evolution of language attitude research needs refining by old and new general attitude theory and research.

There is a contention implicit in the belief that general attitude theory and research form an important foundation for the study of language attitudes. The contention is that the dominant approach to language attitudes thus far has often been sociolinguistic. A complementary social psychological approach partly rooted in general attitude theory and research has theoretical insights to enrich minority language studies.

At the same time, language attitudes are just one component among many in the overall, universal study of minority and majority languages.

In Giles, Leets & Coupland's (1990) overarching framework of minority language processes at an individual and societal level, one major component is termed Sociostructural Perceptions. For Giles *et al.* (1990) 'different people have different fluctuating views about the vitality of their group and its language *vis-à-vis* relevant others. The stronger the perceived sociostructural support for the language among the group and beyond it, the more it may seem worthwhile investing energy in supporting it' (p. 42). Those seeking to link the themes of this book to such a unifying framework may find that such themes relate to Giles *et al.*'s (1990) Sociostructural Perceptions.

The second issue or deficiency was defined as the lack of reference to attitude change theory and research in language attitude writings. Chapter 5 sought to examine the relevance of attitude change (from within social psychology) to individual language shift. As distinct from dominant sociolinguistic approaches, this analysis starts at the level of the individual rather than at societal level. As different from dominant approaches to minority language shift, language planning, language status and language restoration (e.g. Fishman, 1990) which start and end their analysis at a group level, the complementary approach of this book has been to look at change at an individual level. To illustrate: Fishman's (1990) eight stages of Reversing Language Shift examine how minority languages may move through a graded series of priorities to revive or restabilise a minority language. This perceptive analysis is at the level of language communities, neighbourhoods, generations, populations, communities, schools, work spheres, local government services and cultural institutions.

Much of Chapter 5 and the research approach taken in this book focused instead at the person level. There is nothing superior or inferior about taking an individual or societal approach. Ultimately they are entwined and bonded together. The psychological perspective of this book is found in, for example, the discussion of utilitarian functions, knowledge, ego defense and value-expressive functions of attitudes, in the insights from classical conditioning, operant conditioning and human modelling theory, and in various consistency theories from social psychology. Locating attitude change at the person level acknowledges the social, interpersonal nature of attitude change. No person is an island. Attitudes are socially derived and often socially modified. Contextual influences can be employed at the individual level of analysis as effects on an individuals functioning and not purely as effects on group language shift.

The analysis of attitude change at an individual level draws its substance from a wide variety of theoretical perspectives; therefore no overarching theory or model is offered. Rather the perspective taken in this book suggests a variety of conditions (internal to the person and external) that enhances or decreases the probability of attitude change. Drawn from varied psychological and social psychological theories and from attitude research, the canvas depicted in Chapter 5 provides a wide set of statements about potential individual attitude change.

The three remaining issues addressed by the book were investigated by research. The concern for reliable measurement, exploration of multidimensionality (or unidimensionality) of measuring scales and the preference for inter-relating all variables in an overall model has been exemplified in Chapters 3, 4 and 6. These chapters also sought by research to advance understanding of the origins of language attitudes and to construct a holistic attitude to bilingualism scale.

The results of the 'origins of language attitudes research' suggested that at the age of 13 and 14 (third year in secondary school) a major structural shift in attitudes takes place. While younger children express favourable attitudes to a minority language, as the teenage years commence, positive attitudes to a minority language decline. What happens at the onset of the teenage years to cause change? Puberty and physiological changes? Adolescence as a period of storm and stress? The development of abstract thinking (e.g. Piaget's formal operations period)? The shift away from a family based existence to one centred more on the peer group? The influence of the mass media? The development of the peer group as an orientation towards adulthood? Heterosexual relationships? The need for a unified self concept, self esteem and self enhancement? Further research needs to probe such questions. To pose possible causes of language attitude change is not solely a theoretical or research issue. Causes of decline in positive attitude to minority languages are an issue of policy and provision. Answers to questions about causes may lead directly to strategies for language maintenance.

The mere list of questions indicates that locating causes will be difficult. The answers will not be simple. The factors that evoke change are likely to be many and varied, complex and interacting. Simple recipes will fail to capture the variety of chemical actions and reactions that occur. However, from the research analyses and the chapter on attitude change, some clear pointers emerge.

In the early teenage years, there may be a change in what is pleasurably rewarding in an operant and classical conditioning sense. What is essential for the ego and self esteem is re-examined. Among those whose language attitudes change, status and self esteem seem increasingly to come from the culture initially experienced in the early teens. Discos, pop music, pop stars, spending time with a peer group, starting to form heterosexual relationships become events of the teens rather than of childhood.

The rewards of peer group conformity and culture may affect values and attitudes. The mega star rarely belongs to the minority language; the 'top of the charts' group or singer performs in a majority language; the models that many teenagers emulate from the screen rarely speak or represent a minority language. To be consistent, a teenager may have to reject minority language values to take on the values of the peer group.

The danger is in stereotyping. All teenagers do not fit into this pattern. Of particular interest in this research was those whose language attitudes stayed favourable into the teenage years. Not all teenagers become less favourable in their attitude to a minority language. The key factor in maintenance appears to be not engaging in the 'popular' peer culture. Rather such teenagers chose continuity in culture. Having a minority language background and involvement in minority language cultural events provided the anchor to retain a favourable attitude to the minority language.

The research suggests that a crucial event is whether the early teenager stays with, or moves away from, minority language cultural activity. What appears critical is whether minority language events stay rewarding and self enhancing. For many, minority language events do not provide the rewards, status and self enhancement desired. For others, there is reinforcement and self esteem to be gained from minority language activities.

What do such results say about the fate of a minority language? A minority language will find difficulty in bunkering itself against the influence of majority language, popular mass-media culture, or against peer groups operating through the majority language. A bunker attitude to a minority language stands the risk of being the death of that language. A few zealots will remain; the majority will probably want to be in the global village and not an isolation ward.

For minority language attitudes to stay favourable, the reward systems and the cultural forms available must be continually revised and modernised. The widest range of cultural options needs to be available. A menu restricted to language lessons in school is a diet for the few. The menu needs to include a constant re-interpretation of minority language cultural forms. Minority language discos and dating, minority language rock bands and records, minority language books and beer festivals become as important as traditional cultural forms. Teenagers who actively participate in a minority language in the years of rapid personal and social change are those who are more likely to retain positive attitudes. Speaking a minority language while passing a rugby ball, passing a kiss, on the ski slope or in the fast food shop becomes important.

In the last analysis, language planning can provide the conditions and contexts but cannot convince or obtain conformity. There is no easy, workable solution to offsetting or countering the effects of majority language 'popular' culture. The research has shown the age group and their activities which pose a challenge. Efforts to provide a tantalising menu of opportunities and experiences in the early teenage years for minority language speakers are as important as the efforts of bilingual education.

Whether a minority language lives or dies may be about its ability to give a life-saving injection to the culture of its teenagers. The life support machines of language Acts and agencies are only valuable if minority language culture in teenage years is alive and fed with new ideas and initiatives. When the language is lost in the teens and early twenties, it may be lost forever.

If there is a theme of the book that is a beginning, it is attitude to bilingualism. Attitude to a minority language has until now been a focus in minority language research. An attempt has been made at a conceptual and measurement level to delineate attitude to bilingualism as an holistic, additive and organic variable. A unidimensional scale to measure attitude to bilingualism has been derived and tested for internal reliability and validity. This is just the initial exploration. The scale needs testing with different samples varying in age and context. The value of attitude to bilingualism in policy making and as part of a wider theory of minority and majority language life needs further assessment and amplification.

While languages in conflict is a popular and negative theme, the assumption of the attitude to bilingualism theme is that the positive integration and relatively harmonic co-existence of languages within an individual is also worthy of consideration. While bilingualism at an individual and societal level may be in a constant state of change, this is not to suppose continuous conflict and contention. Within the evolution and development of languages within an individual and within society can be a view of bilingualism as a unified entity. Bilingualism as a language.

Appendix 1: The Research Instruments: English and Welsh Versions

PART ONE

Listed below are some of the things people of your age do when not in school.
Please answer each one in terms of whether **you** do these

VERY OFTEN
FAIRLY OFTEN
SOMETIMES
RARELY
NEVER

(tick ✓ your chosen answer)

	VERY OFTEN (5)	FAIRLY OFTEN (4)	SOME-TIMES (3)	RARELY (2)	NEVER (1)
1. Go to a Youth Club					
2. Go to a Church/Chapel					
3. Play Sport					
4. Watch T.V./Videos					
5. Read Newspapers					
6. Read Books out of school					
7. Read magazines/comics					
8. Go to Discos					
9. Go to Yr Urdd					
10. Part-time Work					
11. Play Records/Cassettes					
12. Visit Relatives					
13. A Hobby					
14. Go to Eisteddfodau					
15. Spend time with Boys of my age					
16. Spend time with Girls of my age					
17. Shopping					
18. Walking					
19. Go to a Library					
20. Do nothing very much					

PART TWO

Here are some questions about the language in which you talk to different people, and the language in which certain people speak to you. Please answer as honestly as possible. There are no right or wrong answers. Leave an empty space if a question does not fit your position.

In which language do YOU speak to the following people? Choose one of these answers:

Always in Welsh
In Welsh more often than English
In Welsh and English about equally
In English more often than Welsh
Always in English

	ALWAYS IN WELSH	IN WELSH MORE OFTEN THAN ENGLISH	IN WELSH AND ENGLISH EQUALLY	IN ENGLISH MORE OFTEN THAN WELSH	ALWAYS IN ENGLISH
1. Father					
2. Mother					
3. Brothers/Sisters					
4. Friends in the Classroom					
5. Friends outside School					
6. Teachers					
7. Friends in the Playground					
8. Neighbours (near my house)					
	(5)	(4)	(3)	(2)	(1)

In which language do the following people speak to you?

	ALWAYS IN WELSH	IN WELSH MORE OFTEN THAN ENGLISH	IN WELSH AND ENGLISH EQUALLY	IN ENGLISH MORE OFTEN THAN WELSH	ALWAYS IN ENGLISH
1. Father					
2. Mother					
3. Brother/Sisters					
4. Friends in the Classroom					
5. Friends outside School					
6. Teachers					
7. Friends in the Playground					
8. Neighbours (near my house)					
	(5)	(4)	(3)	(2)	(1)

Which language do YOU use with the following?

	ALWAYS IN WELSH	IN WELSH MORE OFTEN THAN ENGLISH	IN WELSH AND ENGLISH EQUALLY	IN ENGLISH MORE OFTEN THAN WELSH	ALWAYS IN ENGLISH
1. Watching T.V./Videos					
2. Church/Chapel					
3. Newspapers/Comics/Magazines					
4. Records/Cassettes					
5. Radio					
	(5)	(4)	(3)	(2)	(1)

PART THREE

How **important or unimportant** do you think the Welsh language is for people to do the following? There are no right or wrong answers.

FOR PEOPLE TO:

	IMPORTANT (4)	A LITTLE IMPORTANT (3)	A LITTLE UNIMPORTANT (2)	UNIMPORTANT (1)
1. To make friends				
2. To earn plenty of money				
3. Read				
4. Write				
5. Watch T.V./Videos				
6. Get a job				
7. Become cleverer				
8. Be liked				
9. Live in Wales				
10. Go to Church/Chapel				
11. Sing (e.g. with others)				
12. Play sport				
13. Bring up children				
14. Go shopping				
15. Make phone calls				
16. Pass exams				
17. Be accepted in the community				
18. Talk to friends in school				
19. Talk to teachers in school				
20. Talk to people out of school				

Here are some statements about the <u>Welsh language.</u> Please say whether you **agree or disagree** with these statements. There are no right or wrong answers. Please be as honest as possible. Answer with ONE of the following:

SA = Strongly Agree	(circle **SA**)
A = Agree	(circle **A**)
NAND = Neither Agree Nor Disagree	(circle **NAND**)
D = Disagree	(circle **D**)
SD = Strongly Disagree	(circle **SD**)

_{(5)   (4)   (3)   (2)   (1)}

1. I like hearing Welsh spoken...SA A NAND D SD

2. I prefer to watch T.V. in English than Welsh......................................SA A NAND D SD

3. Welsh should be taught to all pupils in Wales...................................SA A NAND D SD

4. Its a waste of time to keep the Welsh language alive......................SA A NAND D SD

5. I like speaking Welsh...SA A NAND D SD

6. Welsh is a difficult language to learn..SA A NAND D SD

7. There are more useful languages to learn than Welsh...................SA A NAND D SD

8. I'm likely to use Welsh as an adult..SA A NAND D SD

9. Welsh is a language worth learning...SA A NAND D SD

10. Welsh has no place in the modern world..SA A NAND D SD

11. Welsh will disappear as everyone in Wales
can speak English...SA A NAND D SD

12. Welsh is essential to take part fully in Welsh life............................SA A NAND D SD

13. We need to preserve the Welsh language......................................SA A NAND D SD

14. Children should not be made to learn Welsh..................................SA A NAND D SD

15. I would like Welsh to take over from the English
language in Wales...SA A NAND D SD

16. It's hard to study Science in Welsh...SA A NAND D SD

17. You are considered a lower class person
if you speak Welsh..SA A NAND D SD

18. I prefer to be taught in Welsh...SA A NAND D SD

19. As an adult, I would like to marry a Welsh speaker........................SA A NAND D SD

20. If I have children, I would like them to be
Welsh speaking..SA A NAND D SD

Here are some statements about the <u>English and Welsh language.</u> Please say whether you **agree or disagree** with these statements. There are no right or wrong answers. Please be as honest as possible. Answer with ONE of the following:

SA = Strongly Agree	(circle **SA**)
A = Agree	(circle **A**)
NAND = Neither Agree Nor Disagree	(circle **NAND**)
D = Disagree	(circle **D**)
SD = Strongly Disagree	(circle **SD**)

(5)   (4)   (3)   (2)   (1)

1. It is important to be able to speak English and Welsh..........SA A NAND D SD

2. To speak one language in Wales is all that is needed.........SA A NAND D SD

3. Knowing Welsh and English makes people cleverer...........SA A NAND D SD

4. Children get confused when learning English_and Welsh...SA A NAND D SD

5. Speaking both Welsh and English helps to get a job..........SA A NAND D SD

6. Being able to write in English and Welsh is important.........SA A NAND D SD

7. All schools in Wales should teach pupils to speak in
Welsh and English...SA A NAND D SD

8. Road signs should be in English and Welsh.........................SA A NAND D SD

9. Speaking two languages is not difficult.................................SA A NAND D SD

10. Knowing both Welsh and English gives people problems.SA A NAND D SD

11. I feel sorry for people who cannot speak both
English and Welsh..SA A NAND D SD

12. Children in Wales should learn to read in
both Welsh and English..SA A NAND D SD

13. People know more if they speak English and Welsh.........SA A NAND D SD

14. People who speak Welsh and English can have more
friends than those who speak one language......................SA A NAND D SD

15. Speaking both English and Welsh is more for older
than younger people..SA A NAND D SD

SA = Strongly Agree   (circle **SA**)
A = Agree   (circle **A**)
NAND = Neither Agree Nor Disagree   (circle **NAND**)
D = Disagree   (circle **D**)
SD = Strongly Disagree   (circle **SD**)

                            (5)   (4)   (3)   (2)   (1)

16. Speaking both Welsh and English helps people
get promotion in their job...SA A NAND D SD

17. Young children learn to speak Welsh and English at the
same time with ease...SA A NAND D SD

18. Both English and Welsh should be important in Wales......SA A NAND D SD

19. People can earn more money if they speak both
Welsh and English...SA A NAND D SD

20. I should not like English to take over from the
Welsh language..SA A NAND D SD

21. When I become an adult, I would like to be considered
as a speaker of English and Welsh..SA A NAND D SD

22. All people in Wales should speak Welsh and English..........SA A NAND D SD

23. If I have children, I would want them to speak both
English and Welsh..SA A NAND D SD

24. Both the Welsh and English languages can live
together in Wales...SA A NAND D SD

25. People only need to know one language..............................SA A NAND D SD

PART SIX

1. **AGE:**   ...... years old

2. **YEAR IN SCHOOL:**   ...... 3rd Year
                              ...... 4th. Year
                              ...... 5th. Year

3. **GENDER**   ...... Male

                     ...... Female

4. How well do YOU think YOU compare with other children of your age in your school.

(a) in **MATHS**

Near the top..............
Better than average.......
About average.............
Below the average.........
Near the bottom..........

(b) in being able to speak **WELSH** (even if you no longer have Welsh language lessons)

Near the top..............
Better than average.......
About average.............
Below the average.........
Near the bottom..........

5.   SURNAME...................   CHRISTIAN NAME(S) ....

RHAN UN

Rhestrir isod rai o'r pethau y bydd pobl ieuanc o'ch oedran chi yn wneud pan nad ydynt yn yr ysgol. Gan ddefnyddio un o'r termau yma, wnewch chi os gwelwch yn dda ddweud a fyddech **chi** yn gwneud y pethau hyn

YN AML IAWN
YN WEDDOL AML
WEITHIAU
ANAML
BYTH
(Rhowch √ i ddangos eich dewis)

	YN AML IAWN	YN WEDDOL AML	WEITHIAU	ANAML	BYTH
	(5)	(4)	(3)	(2)	(1)
1. Mynd i Glwb Ieuenctid					
2. Mynd i Eglwys/Gapel					
3. Chwarae Gemau					
4. Gwylio'r Teledu/Fideo					
5. Darllen Papurau Newyddion					
6. Darllen llyfrau y tu-allan i'r ysgol					
7. Darllen cylchgronau /comics					
8. Mynd i ddiscos					
9. Mynd i'r Urdd					
10. Gweithio rhan-amser					
11. Chwarae recordiau/casetiau					
12. Ymweld â pherthnasau					
13. Ymddiddori mewn hobi					
14. Mynd i Eisteddfodau					
15. Gwario amser efo hogiau o'r un oed â mi					
16. Gwario amser efo merched o'r un oed â mi					
17. Siopa					
18. Cerdded					
19. Mynd i lyfrgell					
20. Yn gwneud fawr ddim					
21. Yn bwyta 'allan' efo'r teulu					
22. Yn mynd ar deithiau efo'r teulu					
23. Yn mynd i theatr/sinema efo'r teulu					
24. Yn mynd ar fy ngwyliau efo'r teulu					
25. Yn mwynhau gweithgareddau awyr agored neu chwaraeon efo'r teulu					

RHAN DAU

Dyma gwestiynnau am yr **iaith** a fyddech yn siarad â rhai pobl, ac am yr **iaith** fydd rhai pobl yn siarad â chi. Atebwch mor onest ag y medrwch. Nid oes atebion cywir nac anghywir. Gadewch unrhyw gwestiwn os nad yw'n berthnasol i chi.

Ym mha iaith ydych CHI yn siarad a'r bobl a ganlyn? Dewiswch un o'r atebion yma.

Yn Gymraeg bob amser
Yn Gymraeg am amlach na Saesneg
Yn Gymraeg yn gymaint a Saesneg
Yn Saesneg yn fwy na Chymraeg
Yn Saesneg bob amser

(Rhowch √ i ddangos eich hateb)

	Yn Gymraeg bob amser (5)	Yn Gymraeg yn amlach na Saesneg (4)	Yn Gymraeg yn gymaint a Saesneg (3)	YnSaesneg yn fwy na Chymraeg (2)	Yn Saesneg bob amser (1)
1. Tad					
2. Mam					
3. Brodyr/Chwiorydd					
4. Ffrindiau yn y dosbarth					
5. Ffrindiau o'r tu-allan i'r ysgol					
6. Athrawon					
7. Ffrindiau ar iard yr ysgol					
8. Cymdogion (gerllaw fy nghartref)					

Ym mha iaith y mae'r bobl a ganlyn yn siarad â chi?

	Yn Gymraeg bob amser (5)	Yn Gymraeg yn amlach na Saesneg (4)	Yn Gymraeg yn gymaint a Saesneg (3)	YnSaesneg yn fwy na Chymraeg (2)	Yn Saesneg bob amser (1)
1. Tad					
2. Mam					
3. Brodyr/Chwiorydd					
4. Ffrindiau yn y dosbarth					
5. Ffrindiau o'r tu-allan i'r ysgol					
6. Athrawon					
7. Ffrindiau ar iard yr ysgol					
8. Cymdogion (gerllaw fy nghartref)					

Pa iaith a ddefnyddiwch wrth wneud y canlynol?

	Yn Gymraeg bob amser (5)	Yn Gymraeg yn amlach na Saesneg (4)	Yn Gymraeg yn gymaint a Saesneg (3)	YnSaesneg yn fwy na Chymraeg (2)	Yn Saesneg bob amser (1)
1. Wrth wylio'r teledu/ fideo					
2. Yn yr Eglwys/Capel					
3. Yn darllen papurau newyddion, comics, cylchgronau					
4. Wrth wrando recordiau a chasetiau					
5. Wrth wrando ar y radio					

RHAN TRI

Pa mor bwysig ydych chi'n gredu yw'r **iaith Gymraeg** i bobl wrth wneud y canlynol? Nid oes atebion cywir nac anghywir. (Rhowch ✓ i ddangos eich ateb)

I BOBL WRTH:	PWYSIG (4)	O YCHYDIG BWYS (3)	DIBWYS BRAIDD (2)	DIBWYS (1)
1. Wneud ffrindiau				
2. Ennill pres mawr				
3. Ddarllen				
4. Ysgrifennu				
5. Wylio'r Teledu/Fideo				
6. Gael Swydd				
7. I geisio bod yn fwy galluog (clyfar)				
8. Gael eu hoffi				
9. Fyw yng Nghymru				
10. Fynd i Eglwys/Gapel				
11. Ganu (e.e. gydag eraill)				
12. Chwarae gemau				
13. Fagu plant				
14. Siopa				
15. Ffonio				
16. Lwyddo mewn arholiadau				
17. Gael eu derbyn yn y gymdeithas				
18. Siarad â ffrindiau yn yr ysgol				
19. Siarad ag athrawon				
20. Siarad â phobl o'r tu-allan i'r ysgol				

RHAN PEDWAR

Dyma rai sylwadau am yr iaith Gymraeg. Dwedwch a ydych yn cytuno neu'n anghytuno â'r sylwadau hyn. Nid oes atebion cywir nac anghywir. Byddwch mor onest ag y medrwch. Atebwch ag un o'r canlynol:

C G	=	Cytuno'n Gryf	(cylchu **CG**)
C	=	Cytuno	(cylchu **C**)
HGNA	=	Heb gytuno nac anghytuno	(cylchu **HGNA**)
A	=	Anghytuno	(cylchu **A**)
AG	=	Anghytuno'n Gryf	(cylchu **AG**)

		(5)	(4)	(3)	(2)	(1)
1.	'Rwyn hoffi clywed siarad yn Gymraeg	CG	C	HGNA	A	AG
2.	Gwell gennyf edrych ar deledu yn Gymraeg	CG	C	HGNA	A	AG
3.	Dylasid dysgu Cymraeg i bob plentyn	CG	C	HGNA	A	AG
4.	Gwastraff ar amser yw cadw'r iaith Gymraeg yn fyw	CG	C	HGNA	A	AG
5.	'Rwyn hoffi siarad Cymraeg	CG	C	HGNA	A	AG
6.	Mae'r Gymraeg yn iaith anodd i'w dysgu	CG	C	HGNA	A	AG
7.	Mae ieithoedd mwy defnyddiol na'r Gymraeg i'w dysgu	CG	C	HGNA	A	AG
8.	'Rwyn debyg o ddefnyddio'r Gymraeg wedi tyfu i fyny	CG	C	HGNA	A	AG
9.	Mae'r Gymraeg yn iaith gwerth ei dysgu	CG	C	HGNA	A	AG
10.	Mae lle i'r Gymraeg yn y byd modern	CG	C	HGNA	A	AG
11.	Bydd y Gymraeg yn diflannu gan fod pawb yng Nghymru yn medru siarad Saesneg	CG	C	HGNA	A	AG
12.	Rhaid wrth Gymraeg i fyw bywyd llawn yng Nghymru	CG	C	HGNA	A	AG
13.	Rhaid inni ddiogelu'r iaith Gymraeg	CG	C	HGNA	A	AG
14.	Dylasid gorfodi plant i ddysgu Cymraeg	CG	C	HGNA	A	AG
15.	Carwn weld y Gymraeg yn cymryd lle'r iaith Saesneg yng Nghymru	CG	C	HGNA	A	AG
16.	Mae'n anodd dysgu Gwyddoniaeth drwy'r Gymraeg	CG	C	HGNA	A	AG
17.	Cewch eich ystyried yn berson is-raddol os siaradwch Gymraeg	CG	C	HGNA	A	AG
18.	Gwell gennyf gael fy nysgu drwy'r Gymraeg	CG	C	HGNA	A	AG
19.	Wedi tyfu i fyny carwn briodi un sy'n siarad Cymraeg	CG	C	HGNA	A	AG
20.	Os bydd gennyf blant carwn iddynt fedru siarad Cymraeg	CG	C	HGNA	A	AG

RHAN PUMP

Dyma rai sylwadau am y **Saesneg a'r Gymraeg**. Dywedwch a ydych yn cytuno neu'n anghytuno â'r gosodiadau hyn. Nid oes atebion cywir nac anghywir. Byddwch mor onest ag y medrwch. Atebwch ag UN o'r canlynol:

C G	=	Cytuno'n Gryf	(cylchu **CG**)
C	=	Cytuno	(cylchu **C**)
HGNA	=	Heb gytuno nac anghytuno	(cylchu **HGNA**)
A	=	Anghytuno	(cylchu **A**)
AG	=	Anghytuno'n Gryf	(cylchu **AG**)

	(5)	(4)	(3)	(2)	(1)

1. Mae'n bwysig medru siarad Cymraeg a Saesneg..CG   C   HGNA   A   AG

2. Bydd medru un iaith yn ddigon yng Nghymru ....CG   C   HGNA   A   AG

3. Mae gwybod Cymraeg a Saesneg yn gwneud pobl yn fwy galluog (clyfar).. CG   C   HGNA   A   AG

4. Bydd plant yn drysu wrth ddysgu Cymraeg a Saesneg..CG   C   HGNA   A   AG

5. Bydd siarad Cymraeg a Saesneg yn help i gael swydd..CG   C   HGNA   A   AG

6. Mae medru ysgrifennu'n Saesneg a Chymraeg yn bwysig..CG   C   HGNA   A   AG

7. Dylasai pob ysgol yng Nghymru ddysgu plant i siarad Cymraeg a Saesneg.....................................CG   C   HGNA   A   AG

8. Dylai arwyddion ffyrdd fod yn Gymraeg a Saesneg..CG   C   HGNA   A   AG

9. Nid yw siarad dwy iaith yn anodd ....CG   C   HGNA   A   AG

10. Mae gwybod Cymraeg a Saesneg yn achosi problemau i bobl.....................................CG   C   HGNA   A   AG

11. Drwg gennyf am y bobl sydd heb fedru siarad Saesneg a Chymraeg.................................CG   C   HGNA   A   AG

12. Dylai plant yng Nghymru ddysgu darllen Cymraeg a Saesneg ....CG   C   HGNA   A   AG

13. Bydd pobl yn gwybod mwy os byddant yn siarad Saesneg a Chymraeg.................................CG   C   HGNA   A   AG

14. Bydd gan y rhai sy'n siarad Cymraeg a Saesneg fwy o ffrindiau na'r rhai sydd yn siarad un iaith.................................CG   C   HGNA   A   AG

CG	=	Cytuno'n Gryf	(cylchu **CG**)
C	=	Cytuno	(cylchu **C**)
HGNA	=	Heb gytuno nac anghytuno	(cylchu **HGNA**)
A	=	Anghytuno	(cylchu **A**)
AG	=	Anghytuno'n Gryf	(cy

	(5)	(4)	(3)	(2)	(1)

15. Bydd siarad Saesneg a Chymraeg yn fwy
    dymunol gan hen bobl na phobl ifanc.................................CG   C   HGNA   A   AG

16. Dylai medru siarad Cymraeg a Saesneg
    fod yn help i bawb gael dyrchafiad yn
    eu swyddi...CG   C   HGNA   A   AG

17. Bydd plant bach yn ei chael yn hawdd i ddysgu
    Cymraeg a Saesneg ar yr un pryd.....................................CG   C   HGNA   A   AG

18. Dylai Saesneg a Chymraeg fod yn bwysig
    yng Nghymru..CG   C   HGNA   A   AG

19. Gall pobl ennill rhagor o bres os
    medrant siarad Cymraeg a Saesneg.....................................CG   C HGNA   A   AG

20. Ni charwn weld Saesneg yn cymryd lle'r
    iaith Gymraeg...CG   C   HGNA   A   AG

21. Wedi tyfu i fyny, carwn gael fy ystyried yn un sy'n siarad
    Cymraeg a Saesneg...CG   C   HGNA   A   AG

22. Dylasai pawb yng Nghymru siarad
    Cymraeg a Saesneg ....CG   C   HGNA   A   AG

23. Os bydd gennyf blant, byddwn yn hoffi
    iddynt siarad Saesneg a Chymraeg.....................................CG   C   HGNA   A   AG

24. Gall Cymraeg a Saesneg gyd-fyw yng
    Nghymru ....CG   C   HGNA   A   AG

25. Mae gwybod un iaith yn ddigon i bawb.............................. CG   C   HGNA   A   AG

RHAN CHWECH

1. **OED**   ....mlwydd oed

2. **BLWYDDYN YN YR YSGOL** ....y drydedd
                                   ....y bedwaredd
                                   ....y bumed

3. **RHYW**   ....BACHGEN
                                   ....MERCH

4.   Yn eich barn CHI sut **ydych** yn cymharu yn eich gwaith â phlant eraill o'r un oed a chi?

        a) Mewn **MATHEMATEG**

                              Yn agos i'r brig.......................
                              Gwell na'r cyffredin................
                              Canolog...................................
                              Yn is na'r cyffredin.................
                              Yn agos i'r gwaelod..............

        b) Mewn **CYMRAEG**

                              Yn agos i'r brig.......................
                              Gwell na'r cyffredin................
                              Canolog...................................
                              Yn is na'r cyffredin.................
                              Yn agos i'r gwaelod..............

5.   **CEFENW**...................**ENW(AU)**   **BEDYDD**..

Appendix 2: Technical Details of the Research

1. Latent variable analyses were conducted on all scales as outlined in the research chapters. A principal factor analysis as opposed to a principal component analysis was chosen. The latter uses unity in the leading diagonal of the correlation matrix, thus assuming that the correlation and hence the reliability of the item with itself is perfect. This takes no account of unique variance (the sum of the specific variance of a test and its error variance (i.e. unreliability). Thus in principal components, unique variance becomes merged with common variance to give hybrid common latent variables. With Principal Factor analysis, the common variance of an item is estimated. Determination of the number of latent variables to rotate was by the Scree Test (Child, 1970). Where any ambiguity in the Scree Test existed, two or more rotations to simple structure were undertaken. Inspection of the solutions for interpretability and parsimony then decided the number of latent variables. The rotation solutions presented used Varimax. Latent variable analyses using LISREL as part of the model were precluded by the large amount of observrd variables in the initial item pool an by the processing power available.

2. The cluster analyses used a latent class analysis program (for full details see Baker & Hinde, 1984).

3. Reliabilities were assessed by Cronbach's alpha using the weighted Latent variable scales.

4. Some of the basic ideas of the use of LISREL have been presented in the chapters. For the sake of readability and to keep substantial issues to the fore, the technical details of LISREL often found in journal articles have been deliberately excluded from the chapters.

Initial data screening and the production of correlation matrices was by PRELIS (Joreskog & Sorbom, 1988). The maximum likelihood estimation principle was used in LISREL7 to test the models (Joreskog & Sorbom, 1989). The posited model was initially tested, followed by further runs to ensure a statistically acceptable solution (see later) and a parsimonious solution (Everitt, 1984). The examples in Cuttance & Ecob (1988) were particularly helpful in model formulation and testing. Particular attention was paid to the possibility of non-recursiveness in a model and to the importance of plausibility.

The iterations in producing a final model paid attention to: the Chi-Square value (a probability *smaller than* 0.05 suggests that the model is *un*acceptable), the modification indices, T-Values, Normalised residuals and the residualised correlation matrix (Luijben, 1989). With the exception of the instrumental attitude model, the requirements of the above criteria were 'satisfied' by the final models.

With the attitude change LISREL models, a longitudinal model was adopted (Hendrickson and Jones, 1989). A longitudinal LISREL model avoids the use of simple 'difference', 'change' or 'gain' scores. Such a model also incorporates residualised scores without their initial calculation (Hendrickson & Jones, 1988).

Details of the final models are given on the following pages.

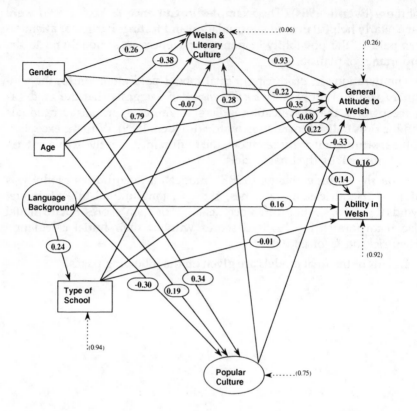

Model 1: General Attitude to Welsh

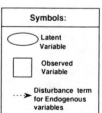

Chi-square = 5.89 ; d.f.=6; p=0.44

Squared Multiple Correlation for General Attitude to Welsh = 0.87

Squared Multiple Correlation for Structural Equations = 0.74

Total Coefficient of Determination for Structural Equations = 0.93

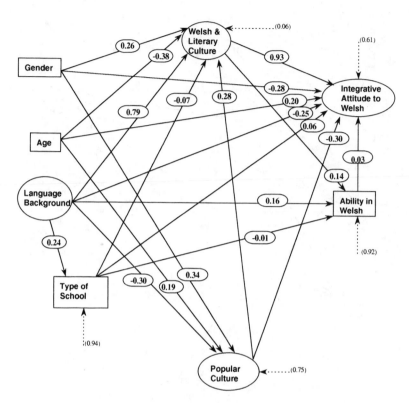

Model 2: Integrative Attitude to Welsh

Chi-square = 5.89 ; d.f.=6; p=0.44

Squared Multiple Correlation for Integrative Attitude = 0.85

Squared Multiple Correlation for Structural Equations = 0.39

Total Coefficient of Determination for Structural Equations = 0.90

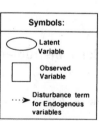

Symbols:

Latent Variable

Observed Variable

Disturbance term for Endogenous variables

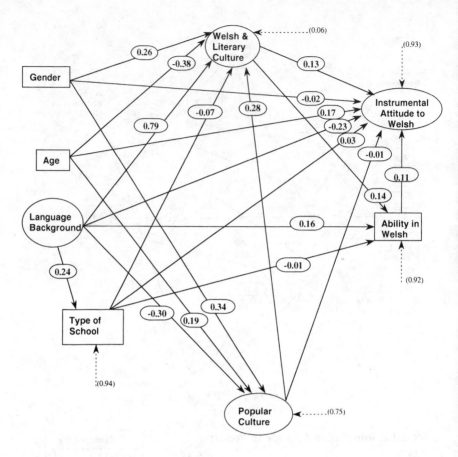

Model 3: Instrumental Attitude to Welsh

Chi-square = 6.49 ; d.f.=6; p=0.37

Squared Multiple Correlation for Instrumental Attitude = 0.77

Squared Multiple Correlation for Structural Equations = 0.07

Total Coefficient of Determination for Structural Equations = 0.95

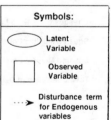

Symbols:

⬭ Latent Variable

▭ Observed Variable

···▶ Disturbance term for Endogenous variables

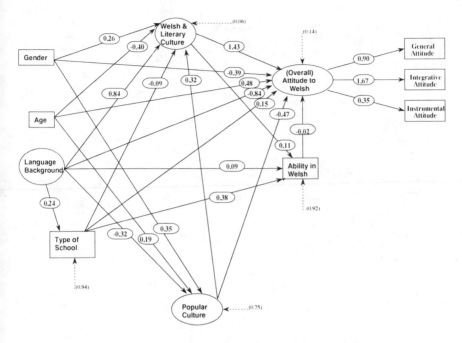

Model 4: An Overall Attitude Model

Model analyzed by the Two Stage Least Squares Estimation Method

Squared Multiple Correlation for Attitude to Welsh = 1.00

Squared Multiple Correlation for Structural Equations = 0.66

Total Coefficient of Determination for Structural Equations = 0.97

Symbols:

◯ Latent Variable

☐ Observed Variable

---▶ Disturbance term for Endogenous variables

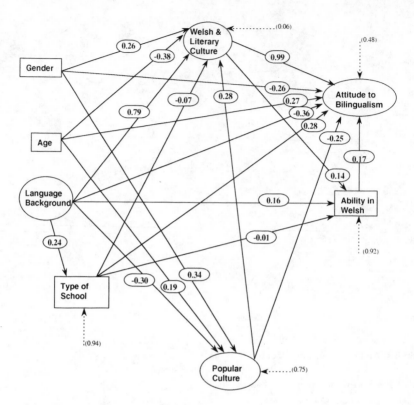

Model 5: Attitude to Bilingualism

Chi-square = 5.68 ; d.f.=6; p=0.46

Squared Multiple Correlation for Attitude to Bilingualism = 0.80

Squared Multiple Correlation for Structural Equations = 0.52

Total Coefficient of Determination for Structural Equations = 0.89

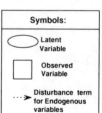

Longitudinal Change Models (Chapter 6)

List of Variables	Symbol
Gender	X1
Age	X2
Language Background and School	X3
Welsh & Literary Culture (first testing)	Y1
Popular Culture (first testing)	Y2
Attitude (first testing)	Y3
(a) to Bilingualism	
(b) to Welsh (general)	
(c) Uses and Functions of Welsh (composite)	
Ability in Welsh (first testing)	Y4
Welsh & Literary Culture (second testing)	Y5
Popular Culture (second testing)	Y6
Attitude (second testing)	Y7
(a) to Bilingualism	
(b) to Welsh (general)	
(c) Uses of Welsh	
Ability in Welsh (second testing)	Y8

Attitude to Bilingualism (Change Model)

Gamma Matrix	X1	X2	X3
Y1	0.28	–0.25	0.49
Y2	0.31	0.14	–0.23
Y3	–0.07	0.00	0.21
Y4	0.00	0.00	0.13
Y5	0.20	0.00	0.00
Y6	–0.16	0.03	0.06
Y7	0.11	0.00	0.14
Y8	0.00	0.00	0.18

Beta Matrix	Y1	Y2	Y3	Y4	Y5	Y6	Y7	Y8
Y1	0.00	0.00	0.00	0.00	0.00	0.00	0.00	0.00
Y2	0.00	0.00	0.00	0.00	0.00	0.00	0.00	0.00
Y3	0.23	0.00	0.00	0.12	0.00	0.00	0.00	0.00
Y4	0.09	–0.05	0.00	0.00	0.00	0.00	0.00	0.00
Y5	0.05	0.89	–0.06	0.00	0.00	0.00	0.00	0.00
Y6	0.65	–1.3	0.05	0.11	1.35	0.00	0.00	0.00
Y7	–0.23	0.92	0.39	–0.09	–0.95	0.40	0.00	0.23
Y8	0.09	–0.26	0.07	0.17	0.26	0.05	0.00	0.00

Chi-square = 4.41; d.f. = 3; p = 0.220
Squared Multiple Correlation (attitude to Bilingualism) = 0.90
Squared Multiple Correlation for Structural Equations= 0.45
Total Coefficient of Determination = 0.61

General Attitude to Welsh (Change Model)

Gamma Matrix	X1	X2	X3
Y1	0.29	–0.26	0.50
Y2	0.31	0.15	–0.23
Y3	–0.06	0.00	0.37
Y4	0.00	0.00	0.13
Y5	0.20	0.00	0.00
Y6	–0.23	0.05	0.05
Y7	0.29	0.00	0.18
Y8	0.00	0.00	0.16

Beta Matrix	Y1	Y2	Y3	Y4	Y5	Y6	Y7	Y8
Y1	0.00	0.02	0.00	0.00	0.00	0.00	0.00	0.00
Y2	0.00	0.00	0.00	0.00	0.00	0.00	0.00	0.00
Y3	0.23	–0.07	0.00	0.12	0.00	0.00	0.00	0.00
Y4	0.09	–0.05	0.00	0.00	0.00	0.00	0.00	0.00
Y5	0.04	0.90	0.00	0.00	0.00	0.00	0.00	0.00
Y6	0.69	–1.54	0.00	0.12	1.6	0.00	0.00	0.00
Y7	–0.28	1.42	0.37	–0.09	–1.52	0.52	0.00	0.19
Y8	0.09	–0.28	0.10	0.17	0.28	0.04	0.00	0.00

Chi-square = 4.36; d.f. = 3; p = 0.225
Squared Multiple Correlation (attitude to Welsh) = 0.90
Squared Multiple Correlation for Structural Equations = 0.53
Total Coefficient of Determination = 0.71

Attitude to the Use of Welsh (Change Model)

Gamma Matrix	X1	X2	X3
Y1	0.28	–0.25	0.48
Y2	0.31	0.15	–0.23
Y3	–0.04	–0.03	0.17
Y4	0.00	0.00	0.13
Y5	0.21	0.00	0.00
Y6	–0.28	0.06	0.04
Y7	0.05	0.00	0.27
Y8	0.00	0.00	0.19

Beta Matrix	Y1	Y2	Y3	Y4	Y5	Y6	Y7	Y8
Y1	0.00	0.02	0.00	0.00	0.00	0.00	0.00	0.00
Y2	0.00	0.00	0.00	0.00	0.00	0.00	0.00	0.00
Y3	0.25	–0.04	0.00	0.03	0.00	0.00	0.00	0.00
Y4	0.09	–0.05	0.00	0.00	0.00	0.00	0.00	0.00
Y5	0.00	0.90	0.03	0.00	0.00	0.00	0.00	0.00
Y6	0.81	–1.66	–0.12	0.12	1.72	0.00	0.00	0.00
Y7	–0.16	0.48	0.10	–0.00	–0.51	0.40	0.00	0.19
Y8	0.11	–0.27	0.00	0.18	0.26	0.00	0.00	0.00

Chi-square = 4.38; d.f. = 3; p = 0.223
Squared Multiple Correlation (attitude to Use of Welsh) = 0.90
Squared Multiple Correlation for Structural Equations = 0.25
Total Coefficient of Determination = 0.70

Disturbance Terms for the Attitude Change Models

1. Attitude to Bilingualism (Change Model)

Y1	0.68
Y2	0.90
Y3	0.83
Y4	0.95
Y5	0.07
Y6	0.15
Y7	0.55
Y8	0.82

2. General Attitude to Welsh (Change Model)

Y1	0.68
Y2	0.90
Y3	0.83
Y4	0.95
Y5	0.07
Y6	0.15
Y7	0.47
Y8	0.82

3. Attitude to the Use of Welsh (Change Model)

Y1	0.68
Y2	0.90
Y3	0.83
Y4	0.95
Y5	0.07
Y6	0.15
Y7	0.75
Y8	0.82

References

Abelson, R.P. 1988, Conviction. *American Psychologist* 43, 267– 75.

Ajzen, I. 1988, *Attitudes, Personality and Behaviour*. Milton Keynes: Open University Press.

Ajzen, I. and M. Fishbein. 1980, *Understanding Attitudes and Predicting Social Behaviour*. New Jersey: Prentice-Hall.

Allport, G.W. 1935, Attitudes. In C. Murchison (ed.) *A Handbook of Social Psychology*. Worcester, Mass.: Clark University Press.

Argyle, M. 1983, *The Psychology of Interpersonal Behaviour*. Harmondsworth, Middlesex: Penguin.

Aronson, E. 1980, *The Social Animal*. San Francisco: W.H. Freeman.

Au, S.Y. 1984, Social psychological variables in second language learning. Unpublished M.Phil. thesis, City University, London.

— 1988, A critical appraisal of Gardner's social-psychological theory of second-language (L2) learning. *Language Learning* 38(1), 75–100.

Bain, B. and Yu, A. 1984, The development of the body percept among working- and middle-class unilinguals and bilinguals. In M. Paradis and Y. Lebrun (eds) *Early Bilingualism and Child Development*. Lisse, Holland: Swets and Zeitlinger.

Baker, C.R. 1976, Affiliation motivation: A psychological examination of some aspects of its origins, nature and effects. Unpublished Ph.D.thesis, University of Wales.

— 1985, *Aspects of Bilingualism in Wales*. Clevedon: Multilingual Matters.

— 1988, *Key Issues in Bilingualism and Bilingual Education*. Clevedon: Multilingual Matters.

— 1990a, The growth of bilingual education in the secondary schools of Wales. In W.G. Evans (ed.) *Perspectives on a Century of Secondary Education in Wales 1889–1989*. Aberystwyth: Y Ganolfan Astudiaethau Addysg.

— 1990b, The effectiveness of bilingual education. *Journal of Multilingual and Multicultural Development* 11(4), 269–77.

Baker, C.R. and Hinde J. 1984, Language background classification. *Journal of Multilingual and Multicultural Development* 5(1), 43– 56.

Baker, C.R. and Waddon, A. 1987, Attitudes of secondary pupils to vandalism. *Collected Original Resources in Education* 11(3), 1– 39.

— 1990, Alcohol: The attitudes and behaviour of young people: A survey of Secondary pupils aged 14 to 17. *Collected Original Resources in Education* 14(1), 1–85.

Bartholomew, D.J. 1987, *Latent Variable Models and Factor Analysis*. London: Griffin.

Bem, D.J. 1967, Self-perception : An alternative interpretation of cognitive dissonance phenomena. *Psychological Review* 74, 183– 200.

— 1968, Attitudes as self-descriptions : Another look at the attitude-behaviour link. In A.G. Greenwald, T.C. Brock and T.M. Ostrom (eds) *Psychological Foundations of Attitudes*. New York: Academic Press.

— 1972, Self perception theory. In L. Berkowitz (ed.) *Advances in Experimental Social Psychology* Vol. 6. New York: Academic Press.

Bourhis, R.Y. and Giles, H. 1977, The language of intergroup distinctiveness. In H. Giles (ed.) *Language, Ethnicity and Intergroup Relations*. London: Academic Press.

Bourhis, R.Y., Giles, H. and Tajfel, H. 1973, Language as a determinant of Welsh identity. *European Journal of Social Psychology* 3, 447–60.

Brown, H. 1981, Affective factors in second language learning. In J. Alatis, H. Altman and P. Alatis (eds) *The Second Language Classroom: Directions for the 1980s*. New York: Oxford University Press.

Burstall, C., Jamieson, M., Cohen, S. and Hargreaves, M. 1974, *Primary French in the Balance*. Windsor: NFER/Nelson.

Cacioppo, J.T. and Petty, R.E. 1982, Language variables, attitudes and persuasion. In E.B. Ryan and H. Giles (eds) *Attitudes Towards Language Variation*. London: E. Arnold.

Child, D. 1970, *The Essentials of Factor Analysis*. London: Holt, Rinehart and Winston.

CILAR (Committee on Irish Language Attitudes Research) 1975, *Report of the Committee on Irish Language Attitudes Research*. Dublin: Government Stationery Office.

Cooper, J. and Croyle, R.T. 1984, Attitudes and attitude change. *Annual Review of Psychology* 35, 395–426.

Cooper, J.B. and McGaugh, J.L. 1966, Attitude and related concepts. In M. Jahoda and N. Warren (eds) *Attitudes*. Harmondsworth, Middlesex: Penguin.

Cuttance, P. and Ecob, R. (eds) 1988, *Structural Modelling by Example*. Cambridge: Cambridge University Press.

Darwin, C. 1872, *The Expression of the Emotions in Man and Animals*. London: Murray.

Davies, B.L. 1988, The right to a bilingual education in nineteenth century Wales. *The Transactions of the Honourable Society of Cymmrodorion* 133–151.

Davies, J.P. 1980, Ymagweddiad disgyblion trydydd dosbarth Ysgolion Uwchradd yng Nghlwyd tuag at y Gymraeg. Unpublished M.Ed. thesis, University of Wales.

— 1986, Dadansoddiad o Nodau Graddedig Ar Gyfer Oedolion Sy'n Dysgu'r Gymraeg Fel Ail Iaith. Unpublished Ph.D. thesis, University of Wales.

Dorian, N. 1981, *Language Death : The Life Cycle of a Scottish Gaelic Dialect*. Philadelphia: University of Pennsylvania Press.

Edwards, J.R. 1977, Students' reactions to Irish regional accents. *Language and Speech* 20, 280–6.

Ellis, R. 1985, *Understanding Second Language Acquisition*. Oxford: Oxford University Press.

Everitt, B.S. 1984, *An Introduction to Latent Variable Models*. London: Chapman & Hall.

Fahy, R.M. 1988, Irish in education: A study of cognitive and affective aspects of achievement in Irish among second-level learners. Ph.D. thesis, University College of Cork, Ireland.

Festinger, L. 1957, *A Theory of Cognitive Dissonance*. Stanford: Stanford University Press.

Festinger, L. and Carlsmith, J.M. 1959, Cognitive consequences of forced compliance. *Journal of Abnormal and Social Psychology* 54, 369–74.

Fishman, J. 1976, *Bilingual Education: An International Sociological Perspective*. Rowley, Mass: Newbury House.

— 1990, What is reversing language shift (RLS) and how can it succeed? *Journal of Multilingual and Multicultural Development* 11(1 & 2), 5–34.

Gardner, R.C. 1979, Social psychological aspects of second language acquisition. In H. Giles and R. St. Clair (eds) *Language and Social Psychology*. Oxford: Blackwell.

— 1981, Second language learning. In R.C. Gardner and R. Kalin (eds) *A Canadian Social Psychology of Ethnic Relations*. London: Methuen.

— 1982, Language attitudes and language learning. In E.B. Ryan and H. Giles (eds) *Attitudes Towards Language Variation*. London: E. Arnold.

— 1983, Learning another language: A true social psychological experiment. *Journal of Language and Social Psychology* 2, 219–39.

— 1985a, *Social Psychology and Second Language Learning*. London: E. Arnold.

— 1985b, *The Attitude/Motivation Test Battery. Technical Report*. Ontario: University of Western Ontario.

— 1988, The socio-educational model of second language learning: Assumptions, findings and issues. *Language Learning* 38(1), 101– 26.

Gardner, R.C., Lalonde, R.N. and MacPherson, J. 1985, Social factors in second language attrition. *Language Learning* 35, 519–40.

Gardner, R.C., Lalonde, R.N. and Moorcroft, R. 1987, Second language attrition: The role of motivation and use. *Journal of Language and Social Psychology* 6(1), 29–47.

Gardner, R.C., Lalonde, R.N. and Pierson, R. 1983, The socio-educational model of second language acquisition: An investigation using LISREL causal modelling. *Journal of Language and Social Psychology* 2, 51–65.

Gardner, R.C. and Lambert, W.E. 1959, Motivational variables in second language acquisition. *Canadian Journal of Psychology* 13, 266–72.

— 1972, *Attitudes and Motivation in Second-Language Learning*. Rowley, Mass.: Newbury House.

Gardner R.C., Moorcroft, R. and Metford, J. 1989, Second language learning in an immersion programme: Factors influencing acquisition and retention. *Journal of Language and Social Psychology* 8(5), 287–305.

Gardner, R.C. and Smythe, P.C. 1975, Second language acquisition: A social psychological approach. *Research Bulletin* 332, University of Western Ontario.

— 1981, On the development of the attitude/motivation test battery. *Canadian Modern Language Review* 37, 510–25.

Genesee, F., Rogers, P. and Holobow, N. 1983, The social psychology of second language learning: Another point of view. *Language Learning* 33(2), 209–24.

Giles, H., Hewstone, M. and Ball, P. 1983, Language attitudes in multilingual settings: Prologue with priorities. *Journal of Multilingual and Multicultural Development* 4(2 & 3), 81–100.

Giles, H., Leets, L. and Coupland, N. 1990, Minority language group status: A theoretical conspexus. *Journal of Multilingual and Multicultural Development* 11 (1 & 2), 37–55.

Gliksman, L. 1976, Second language acquisition: The effects of student attitudes on classroom behaviour. Unpublished M.A. thesis, University of Western Ontario.

— 1981, Improving the prediction of behaviours associated with second language acquisition. Unpublished Ph.D. thesis, University of Western Ontario.

Goldstein, H. 1987, *Multilevel Models in Educational and Social Research*. London: Griffin.

Gordon, M.E. 1980, Attitudes and motivation in second language achievement. Unpublished Ph.D. thesis, University of Toronto.

Grosjean, F. 1985, The bilingual as a competent but specific speaker-hearer. *Journal of Multilingual and Multicultural Development* 6(6), 467–77.

— 1989, Neurolinguists, Beware! The bilingual is not two monolinguals in one person. *Brain and Language* 36, 3–15.

Hamers, J.F. and Blanc, M. 1982, Towards a social-psychological model of bilingual development. *Journal of Language and Social Psychology* 1(1), 29–49.

— 1983, Bilinguality in the young child: A social psychological model. In P.H. Nelde (ed.) *Theory, Methods and Models of Contact Linguistics*. Bonn: Dummler.

— 1989, *Bilinguality and Bilingualism*. Cambridge: Cambridge University Press.

Harre, R., Clarke, D. and De Carlo, N. 1985, *Motives and Mechanisms. An Introduction to the Psychology of Action*. London: Methuen.

Heider, F. 1958, *The Psychology of Interpersonal Relations*. New York: Wiley.

Hendrickson, L. and Jones, B. 1988, A study of longitudinal causal models comparing gain score analysis with structural equation approaches. In P. Cuttance and R. Ecob (eds) *Structural Modelling by Example*. Cambridge: Cambridge University Press.

Herman, S.R. 1968, Explorations in the social psychology of language choice. In J.A. Fishman (ed.) *Readings in the Sociology of Language*. The Hague: Mouton.

Insko, C.A. 1965, Verbal reinforcement of attitudes. *Journal of Personality and Social Psychology* 2, 621–3.

Jahoda, M. and Warren, N. (eds) 1966, *Attitudes*. Harmondsworth, Middlesex: Penguin.

Jaspars, J.M.F. 1978, The nature and measurement of attitudes. In H. Tajfel and C. Fraser (eds) *Introducing Social Psychology*. Harmondsworth, Middlesex: Penguin.

Jones, E.P. 1982, A study of some of the factors which determine the degree of bilingualism of a Welsh child between 10 & 13 years of age. Unpublished Ph.D. thesis, University of Wales.

Jones, T.P. 1990, Migrant pupils: Welsh linguistic implications. *Fourth International Conference on Minority Languages, Volume 2, Western and Eastern European Perspectives* (pp. 91–102). Clevedon: Multilingual Matters.

Jones, W.R. 1949, Attitude towards Welsh as a second language. A preliminary investigation. *British Journal of Educational Psychology* 19(1), 44–52.

— 1950, Attitude towards Welsh as a second language. A further investigation. *British Journal of Educational Psychology* 20(2), 117–32.

— 1966, *Bilingualism in Welsh Education*. Cardiff: University of Wales Press.

Joreskog, K.G. and Sorbom, D. 1988, *PRELIS: A Program for Multivariate Data Screening and Data Summarization. A Preprocessor for LISREL.* Mooresville, Indiana: Scientific Software Inc.

— 1989, *LISREL Users Guide, Version 7.* Mooresville, Indiana: Scientific Software Inc.

Kahle, L.R. 1984, *Attitudes and Social Adaptation.* Oxford: Pergamon.

Katz, D. 1960, The functional approach to the study of attitude. *Public Opinion Quarterly* 24, 163–204.

Kline, P. 1986, *A Handbook of Test Construction.* London: Methuen.

Lalonde, R.N. 1982, Second language acquisition: a causal analysis. Unpublished M.A. thesis, University of Western Ontario.

Lapiere, R.T. 1934, Attitudes versus actions. *Social Forces* 14, 230–7.

Levinson, D.G. 1978, *The Seasons of a Man's Life.* New York: Knopf.

Lewis, E.G. 1975, Attitude to language among bilingual children and adults in Wales. *International Journal of the Sociology of Language* 4, 103–21.

— 1981, *Bilingualism and Bilingual Education.* Oxford: Pergamon.

Lewis, R., Rado, M. and Foster, L. 1982, Secondary school students' attitudes towards bilingual learning in schools. *Australian Journal of Education* 26(3), 292–304.

Likert, R. 1932, A technique for the measurement of attitude. *Archives of Psychology* No. 140.

Linguistic Minorities Project, 1985, *The Other Languages of England.* London: Routledge & Kegan Paul.

Luijben, T.C.W. 1989, *Statistical Guidance for Model Modification in Covariance Structure Analysis.* Amsterdam: Sociometric Research Foundation.

Lukmani, Y.M. 1972, Motivation to learn and learning proficiency. *Language Learning* 22, 261–73.

MacKinnon, K. 1981, Scottish opinion on Gaelic. A report on a national attitude survey for An Comunn Gaidhealach. Hatfield Polytechnic, Social Science Research Publication No. 5514.

Marsh, C. 1982, *The Survey Method. The Contribution of Surveys to Sociological Explanation.* London: Allen & Unwin.

McClelland, D.C. 1958, The importance of early learning in the formation of motives. In J.W. Atkinson (ed.) *Motives in Fantasy, Action and Society.* London: Van-Nostrand.

— 1961, *The Achieving Society.* London: Free Press.

McGuire, W.J. 1969, The nature of attitudes and attitude change. In G. Lindzey and E. Aronson (eds) *Handbook of Social Psychology* (2nd edn) Volume 3. Reading, Mass: Addison-Wesley.

McQuire, W.J. 1981, The probabilogical model of cognitive structure and attitude change. In R.E. Petty, T.M. Ostrom and T.C. Brock (eds) *Cognitive Responses in Persuasion.* Hillsdale, NJ: Lawrence Erlbaum.

— 1985, Attitudes and attitude change. In G. Lindzey and E. Aronson (eds) *Handbook of Social Psychology* (3rd edn) Volume 3. New York: Random House.

Mortimore, P. *et al.* 1988, *School Matters: The Junior Years.* Wells: Open Books.

Newcomb, T.M. 1950, *Social Psychology.* New York: Holt.

Naiman, N., Frohlich, M., Stern, H.H. and Todesco, A. 1978, The good language learner. *Research in Education Series No.7*. Ontario Institute for Studies in Education.

Oller, J.W. 1981, Research on the measurement of affective variables. In R. Anderson (ed.) *New Dimensions in L2 Acquisition Research*. Rowley, Mass.: Newbury House.

Oller, J.W., Hudson, A. and Liu, P. 1977, Attitudes and attained proficiency in ESL: A sociolinguistic study of native speakers of Chinese in the United States. *Language Learning* 27, 1–27.

Oller, J.W., Perkins, K. and Murakami, M. 1980, Seven types of learner variables in relation to ESL learning. In J.W. Oller and K. Perkins (eds) *Research in Language Testing*. Rowley, Mass.: Newbury House.

Ó Riagain, P. and Ó Gliasain, M. 1984, *The Irish Language in the Republic of Ireland 1983: Preliminary Report of a National Survey*. Dublin: Instituid Teangeolaiochta Eireann.

Potter, J. and Wetherell, M. 1987, *Discourse and Social Psychology: Beyond Attitudes and Behaviour*. London: Sage.

Ramage, K. 1990, Motivational factors and persistence in foreign language study. *Language Learning* 40(2), 189–219.

Reynolds, D. (ed.) 1985, *Studying School Effectiveness*. London: Falmer Press.

Riley, R.T. and Pettigrew, T.F. 1976, Dramatic events and attitude change. *Journal of Personality and Social Psychology* 34, 1004– 15.

Roberts, C. 1985, Teaching and learning commitment in bilingual schools. Unpublished Ph.D. thesis, University of Wales.

— 1987, Political conflict over bilingual initiatives. *Journal of Multilingual and Multicultural Development* 8(4), 311–22.

Rosenberg, M.J. and Hovland, C.I. 1960, Cognitive, affective and behavioural components of attitudes. In C.I. Hovland and M.J. Rosenberg (eds) *Attitude Organisation and Change*. New Haven: Yale University Press.

Rutter, M. *et al.* 1979, *Fifteen Thousand Hours*. London: Open Books.

Ryan, E.B. 1979, Why do low-prestige language varieties persist? In H. Giles and R.N. St. Clair (eds) *Language and Social Psychology*. Oxford: Blackwell.

Ryan, E.B. and Giles, H. (eds) 1982, *Attitudes Towards Language Variation*. London: E. Arnold.

Saris, W. and Stronkhorst, H. 1984, *Causal Modelling in Nonexperimental Research*. Amsterdam: Sociometric Research Foundation.

Schumann, J.H. 1978, *The Pidginization Process: A Model for Second Language Acquisition*. Rowley, Mass.: Newbury House.

— 1986, Research of the acculturation model for second language acquisition. *Journal of Multilingual and Multicultural Development* 7(5), 379–92.

Sharp, D., Thomas, B., Price, E., Francis, G. and Davies, I.1973, *Attitudes to Welsh and English in the Schools of Wales*. Basingstoke/Cardiff: Macmillan/University of Wales Press.

Shaw, M.E. and Wright, J.M. 1967, *Scales for the Measurement of Attitudes*. New York: McGraw-Hill.

Shipman, M. 1981, *The Limitations of Social Research* (2nd edn). London: Longmans.

Siguan, M. and Mackey, W.F. 1987, *Education and Bilingualism*. London: Kogan Page.

Smith, D.J. and Tomlinson, S. 1989, *The School Effect: A Study of Multi-racial Comprehensives*. London: Policy Studies Institute.

Smith, J.F. 1980, *Language and Language Attitudes in a Bilingual Community*. Leeuwarden: Fryske Akademy.

Spina, J.M. 1979, Adolescent attachment to Canada and commitment to bilingualism. *International Journal of the Sociology of Language* 20, 75–88.

Staats, A. and Staats, C. 1958, Attitudes established by classical conditioning. *Journal of Abnormal and Social Psychology* 57, 37–40.

Strong, M. 1984, Integrative motivation: Cause or result of successful second language acquisition? *Language Learning* 34(3), 1–14.

Svanes, B. 1987, Motivation and cultural distance in second-language acquisition. *Language Learning* 37(3), 341–59.

Tajfel, H. 1981, *Human Groups and Social Categories: Studies in Social Psychology*. Cambridge: Cambridge University Press.

Thomas, C.J. and Williams, C.H. 1977, A behavioural approach to the study of linguistic decline and nationalist resurgence: A case study of the attitudes of sixth formers in Wales. *Cambria* 4(2), 152–73.

Thomas, W.I. and Znaniecki, F. 1918, *The Polish Peasant in Europe and America*. Chicago: University of Chicago Press.

Thurstone, L.L. and Chave, E.J. 1929, *The Measurement of Attitudes*. Chicago: University of Chicago Press.

Triandis, H.C. 1971, *Attitude and Attitude Change*. New York: Wiley.

Wicker, A.W. 1969, Attitudes versus actions: The relationship of verbal and overt behavioural responses to attitude objects. *Journal of Social Issues* 25(4), 41–78.

Williams, C.H. 1986, Bilingual education as an agent in cultural reproduction: Spatial variations in Wales. *Cambria* 13(1), 111–29.

Williams, H.G. 1978, Educational policy and social control: An analysis of policy and policy generators 1846–1870. Unpublished M.Phil. thesis, Brunel University.

Yatim, A.M. 1988, Some factors affecting bilingualism amongst trainee teachers in Malaysia. Unpublished Ph.D. thesis, University of Wales.

Youngman, M.B. 1979, *Analysing Social and Educational Research Data*. London: McGraw-Hill.

Index

Abelson, R.P., 105
Ability, 44, 48f, 61, 89, 122f
Age, 41f, 48f, 61f, 88, 106, 116, 121
Aggregation, 17
Ajzen, I., 11, 13, 15, 16, 20
Allport, G.W., 11
Anxiety, 38f
Aptitude, 38f
Argyle, M., 49
Aronson, E., 104
Asian, 30
Attrition, 36
Au, S.Y., 30, 32

Bain, B., 101
Baker, C.R., 4, 5, 8, 26, 29, 30, 32, 37, 41, 45, 49, 51, 52, 53, 54, 56, 57, 94, 98, 110, 111, 152
Ball, P., 17, 22
Bartholomew, D.J., 56
Behaviour, 15f
Bem, D.J., 11, 104
Bilingualism (Attitude to), 3, 4, 5, 76f, 116, 119f
Blanc, M., 38
Bombay, 34
Bourhis, R.Y, 22, 104
Brown, H., 14
Burstall, C., 30, 34, 41

Cacioppo, J.T., 103
Canada, 77
Carlsmith, J.M., 104
Change (Attitudes), 2, 5, 97f, 114f, 134, 159f
Chave, E.J., 10, 17
Child, D., 152
CILAR (Committee on Irish Language Attitudes Research), 25, 30, 48, 99
Classrooms, 37f
Cluster Analysis, 57f, 65f, 124f, 152
Cohen, S., 30, 34, 41

Community, 107f
Conditioning, 102f
Conformity, 112
Consistency, 104f
Context, 29, 39f, 49f, 63f, 94
Cooper, J., 20
Cooper, J.B., 15
Coupland, N., 134
Cronbach's Alpha 24, 117, 152
Croyle, R.T., 20
Culture, 49
Cuttance, P., 117, 153

Darwin, C., 10
Davies, B.L., 98
Davies, I., 8, 18, 23, 29, 30, 41, 42, 43, 44, 48, 51, 54, 55, 63, 76
Davies, J.P., 29, 48
Definitions, 10f
Disturbance Terms, 73, 74, 94, 154f, 163
Dorian, N., 113
Dramatic Experience, 106

Ecob, R., 117, 153
Edwards, J.R., 22
Ego Defence, 100f
Ellis, R., 14
English, 30, 76
ESRC, v, 49
Everitt, B.S., 153

Fahy, R.M., 30, 48
Festinger, L., 104
Fishbein, M., 13, 20
Fishman, J., 113, 134
Foster, L., 80
Francis, G., 8, 18, 23, 29, 30, 41, 42, 43, 44, 48, 51, 54, 55, 63, 76
French, 30, 32, 77
Frisian, 30
Frohlich, M., 29, 38
Functional Theory, 99f

Gaelic, 30
Gardner R.C., 3, 4, 8, 12, 14, 19, 22, 23,
   24, 30, 32, 33, 34, 35, 36, 37, 38, 39,
   40, 41, 44, 77
Gender, 42, 48f, 61, 88, 120
Genesee, F., 36
Giles, H., 17, 22, 104, 134
Gliksman, L., 29, 37
Goldstein, H., 26, 53
Gordon, M.E., 33
Grosjean, F., 78, 79
Group Discussion, 111f

Hamers, J.F., 38
Hargreaves, M., 30, 34, 41
Harre, R., 9
Heider, F., 104
Hendrickson, L., 153
Herman, S.R., 101
Hewstone, M., 17, 22
Hinde J., 51, 57, 152
Historical Perspectives, 97f
Holobow, N., 36
Hovland, C.I., 13
Hudson, A., 34, 35, 36
Human Modelling, 103f

Ideology, 14
Indoctrination, 112
Inputs, 12, 39
Insko, C.A., 102
Institutions, 110
Instrumental Attitudes, 31f, 56f, 61, 72
Integrative Attitudes, 31f, 56f, 61, 71
Intelligence, 38f
Ireland, 12, 16, 22, 30

Jahoda, M., 11
Jamieson, M., 30, 34, 41
Jaspars, J.M.F., 10, 11
Jones, B., 153
Jones, E.P., 29, 41, 42, 4548, 54, 63, 110
Jones, T.P., 107
Jones, W.R., 23, 24, 29, 30, 31, 41, 42,
   44, 48, 51, 54, 63
Joreskog, K.G., 152

Kahle, L.R., 103
Katz, D., 99, 101
Kline, P., 24
Knowledge Function, 101

Lalonde, R.N., 30, 33, 36, 41, 44
Lambert, W.E., 3, 22, 23, 30, 32, 33, 35,
   77
Language Background, 44, 48f, 57f,
   63f, 92, 116f, 122, 129
Language Loss, 36
Language Retention, 36
Lapiere, R.T., 15
Latent Variable Analysis, 19, 57f, 83f,
   91, 116, 127f, 152
Leets, L., 134
Levinson, D.G., 106
Lewis, E.G., 9, 29, 31, 48, 97
Lewis, R., 80
Likert, R., 17, 25
Linguistic Minorities Project, 51
LISREL, 40, 59, 94, 115, 127, 152, 153
Liu, P., 34, 35, 36
Longitudinal Model, 126f, 159f
Luijben, T.C.W., 153
Lukmani, Y.M., 34

Mackey, W.F., 35, 38
MacKinnon, K., 30, 48
MacPherson, J., 36
Marsh, C., 10
Mass Media, 110f
Matched Guise Technique, 17, 22
McClelland, D.C., 32
McGaugh, J.L., 15
McGuire, W.J., 1, 11, 14, 15, 104, 106,
   109, 110, 111
Metford, J., 37
Modelling, 45f, 68f, 92f, 154f
Moorcroft, R., 33, 37
Mortimore, P., 53, 110
Motivation, 14
Multidimensionality, 2, 8, 18, 24, 30,
   135
Multilevel Analysis, 26, 74
Murakami, M., 36

Naiman, N., 29, 38
Newcomb, T.M., 14
Norwegian, 30

Ó Gliasain, M., 24, 30, 48
Ó Riagain, P., 24, 30, 48
Oller, J.W., 32, 34, 35, 36
Opinion, 10, 14, 30
Outputs, 12, 29

Parents, 109
Peer Groups, 109
Perkins, K. 36
Personality, 15
Pettigrew, T.F., 106
Petty, R.E., 103
Pierson, R., 30, 44
Potter, J., 18
Price, E., 8, 18, 23, 29, 30, 41, 42, 43, 44, 48, 51, 54, 55, 63, 76

Rado, M., 80
Ramage, K., 36
Reliability, 2, 8, 17, 24, 25, 33, 36, 59, 83, 117, 152
Residualized Gain Scores, 120, 124
Reynolds, D., 110
Riley, R.T., 106
Rituals, 111
Roberts, C., 43, 53
Rogers, P., 36
Rosenberg, M.J., 13
Rutter, M., 110
Ryan, E.B., 22, 102

Sampling, 55, 115
Saris, W., 24, 29
Scaling, 23, 55f
School, 43f, 48f, 63, 89f, 121f
Schumann, J.H., 14, 36
Scree Test, 83, 152
Second Language Learning, 33, 34, 35
Self Report, 16
Semantic Differential, 18
Sharp, D., 8, 18, 23, 29, 30, 41, 42, 43, 44, 48, 51, 54, 55, 63, 76
Shaw, M.E., 11, 13
Shipman, M., 28
Siguan, M. 35, 38
Smith, D.J. 53, 110
Smith, J.F., 30
Smythe, P.C., 33, 34
Social Desirability, 19
Sorbom, D., 152
Spina, J.M., 77, 79
Staats, A. 102

Staats, C., 102
Stern, H.H., 29, 38
Strong, M., 34
Stronkhorst, H., 24, 29
Structural Equation Modelling, 2, 5, 19, 40, 50, 74
Suggestion, 111
Svanes, B., 30
Systems Approach, 19, 20, 22, 27

Tajfel, H., 107
Theories (Attitude), 1, 27f, 133
Thomas, B., 8, 18, 23, 29, 30, 41, 42, 43, 44, 48, 51, 54, 55, 63, 76
Thomas, C.J., 29
Thomas, W.I., 10
Thurstone (Scaling Technique), 23
Thurstone, L.L., 10, 17
Todesco, A., 29, 38
Tomlinson, S., 53, 110
Triandis, H.C., 103

Unidimensionality, 24, 30

Validity, 24, 36
Value Expression, 101
Variables, 51f, 115

Waddon A., 51, 53, 54, 56, 111
Warren, N., 11
Welsh Language, 4, 6, 18, 22, 29, 54f, 58f, 76f, 118f, 154f
Wetherell, M., 18
Wicker, A.W., 15
Williams, C.H., 29, 98
Williams, H.G., 98
Wright, J.M., 11, 13, 14

Yatim, A.M., 30
Youngman, M.B., 120
Youth Culture, 45f, 49f, 56f, 65, 89, 116f, 123f, 136
Yu, A., 101

Znaniecki, F., 10